SECOND CORINTHIANS

Michael Ongole

SECOND CORINTHIANS

Ministry:
God at Work in Me
for the Good of Others

Paul F. Bubna

CHRISTIAN PUBLICATIONS
CAMP HILL, PENNSYLVANIA

Christian Publications
3825 Hartzdale Drive, Camp Hill, PA 17011

The mark of ✝ vibrant faith

ISBN: 0-87509-538-0
LOC Catalog Card Number: 93-72165
© 1993 by Christian Publications, Inc.
Printed in the United States of America

93 94 95 96 97 5 4 3 2 1

Cover design by Step One Design

CONTENTS

Life Can Be a Ministry

It happened at a college football game in the eastern United States. At a critical point in the contest the referee assessed a costly penalty against the home team. The coach roared onto the field to protest and when it appeared that the referee was about to waver, the opposing coach joined the fray. The heated discussion degenerated into a pushing and shoving match.

Thousands of spectators witnessed a strange situation. Two football teams in full battle gear were standing on the sidelines watching while two coaches made war on the playing field.

Could this be an apt picture of church life in the 20th century—congregations as cheering sections shouting encouragement to their leaders who do battle on the field? It would appear that for many believers Christian activity consists of going somewhere to watch professional ministers do their thing. Thankfully, a fresh wind of the Holy Spirit has been blowing through the church, awakening millions of saints to the exhilarating awareness that God has gifted every believer and intends for each of us to be ministers of His grace.

The Apostle Paul's second letter to the Corinthian believers is a great resource book for those who want to follow the Spirit-given instincts of the heart and get onto the "playing field." The apostle's first letter was a loving but firm call for correction of the many irregularities in the personal and corporate lifestyle of the Corinthian believers. As is often the case, some in the church answered the call for correction by attacking the caller. A careful reading of this second letter makes it clear that harsh and unfounded criticism was showered upon Paul.

The Second Corinthian letter is Paul's response. The conciliatory note stands in stark contrast. In an attempt to build a bridge of understanding, Paul uncovered his heart and spoke openly of his ministry. The autobiographical nature of the letter allows us to be mentored in ministry by a master teacher. The glad message of Second Corinthians is that for every man or woman who follows Christ in abandonment, life becomes a ministry.

The truth is that the call to follow Christ is a call to ministry. "Come, follow me . . . and I will make you fishers of men" (Matthew 4:19), Jesus said to the fishermen mending their nets.

The dimensions of that call came to light when the mother of James and John came to our Lord requesting a special place for her sons. Her idea was that when Jesus would come into His kingdom her sons would sit at His right and at His left hand. Before we get too critical of her, remember she was only doing what many mothers would have done. But as you might imagine, the other disciples were not thrilled by her motherly ambition.

Jesus rebuked them all:

You know that the rulers of the Gentiles lord it over
them, and their high officials exercise authority over
them. Not so with you. Instead, whoever wants to
become great among you must be your servant, and
whoever wants to be first must be your slave—just
as the Son of Man did not come to be served, but
to serve, and to give his life as a ransom for many.
(20:25–28)

The options are clear. Either we live to be ministered unto,
that is, to manipulate circumstances and people so that we
are served, or else, hearing the call of our Lord, we follow
Him and live for the good of others. It is just this kind of
following that opens the door for life to become a ministry.

Is the life of ministry a sacrifice, a fulfillment, or both?
The opening paragraphs of the letter get right to the heart
of the issue. The salutation is typical of what we might
expect in a first century, mid-eastern letter. However, we
must not pass over it without observation.

Paul identified himself as an apostle of Jesus Christ by the
will of God. The apostolic office was a key factor in the
growth of the New Testament church. Strong leadership
was essential. Paul both affirmed the role he was exercising
and the divine appointment which was the source of
authority. Just because Paul was an apostle and you are not,
don't think that the message of the letter does not apply to
you and your ministry. Offices and gifts may vary but the
dynamics of fruitful ministry are the same.

The Principle of Ministry

The letter begins with praise, a celebration of the character
of God. Paul lauds Him as the Father of compassion and

the God of all comfort. Anything of good or lasting value is rooted in the character of God. That is true of ministry.

I'm aware that we haven't defined the term "ministry" as yet. My intention is that our understanding of ministry will gradually take form as we open the text of Paul's letter. But as a starting point let me offer this definition: Ministry is the supernatural life of God at work in my life in such a way as to bring growth and spiritual fruit in the lives of others.

There are things we can do for needy people that do not involve a transcendent dimension. But touching people's lives in a way that has eternal significance must have its source beyond our fallen human nature. Spiritual ministry flows out of the nature of God. Paul says He is the Father of compassion and the God of all comfort.

Where does ministry begin? God comforts us in all our troubles. He comforts us because it is His character to do so. And what is the nature of this comfort? In the upper room our Lord told His disciples that they would have tribulation in the world. But His word was that they should not be afraid because when He ascended to the Father He would send them another Comforter.

The Holy Spirit is that Comforter. If we are to grasp the message of Second Corinthians, it is essential that we have a clear understanding of the person and work of the Holy Spirit, the third person of the blessed Trinity. He is holy, all-knowing, all-powerful, present everywhere at all times, infinite in wisdom, love and grace. All that the Scriptures declare to be true of the eternal God and Creator is true of the Holy Spirit. When Jesus prepared to return to the Father, He told His disciples that He would send the Holy Spirit, who would be with them and in them (John 14:16–17)—not a force or some sort of energy, but a Person of the Godhead.

What will the Holy Spirit do? Jesus referred to Him as the *Paraclete*, the Comforter. He is the one who walks beside us to make us adequate. All of God's saving work in the believer is wrought by the indwelling presence of the Holy Spirit. It is He who convicts the sinner of his or her need, who brings the new birth in those who believe. And it is He who makes real the things of Christ and illumines the heart and mind of those who seek to obey. It is the Holy Spirit who empowers the believer to obedience and gives victory over temptation. It is by His life that the believer is made holy and finds power to live a holy life.

Our journey through this very personal letter of Paul's will uncover many insights about living in the fullness of God's Spirit. It is the life of the Holy Spirit in the believer that is the source of ministry. In this text Paul says that God comforts us in all our troubles so that we may be a comfort to any who are in trouble.

The Greek word translated "trouble" indicates a heavy burden, a tribulation or a crushing pressure. In ancient England one of the ways that convicts were executed was to lay them on the ground and then pile stones on their chests until the life was literally crushed out of them.

It is not hard to find people whose chests are about to cave in—people with broken hearts, shattered dreams, tragic disappointments, devastating loss and grief. Physical suffering can test our spiritual resources but it is the spiritual and emotional anguish that threatens to cave us in. Failure, guilt, rejection, anger, hatred and bitterness are but a few of the weights that easily get piled on our chests.

So what do you do for people whose chests are caving in? Send them a card, flowers, a basket of fruit? Those helpful acts can all be used to open windows into people's darkness.

But ministry, Paul says, has to do with comforting people with the comfort we have received from God in our troubles.

I have an uncle who has been on a lifelong search for God. He was in our home one evening when I was called to the home of one of the church families where an awful loss had been experienced. When I returned home, he was curious. "Paul, I don't see how you can go into situations like that. What is there to say?"

My response was, "If all you have is words, there is nothing to say." (The fact is that when we are with people in the brunt of awful grief it is usually best to say little or nothing.) The conversation reminded me that just as we have received the life of the Holy Spirit to comfort and make us adequate in our trouble, so that same life of the Holy Spirit is communicated through us to comfort others in their trouble.

The source of spiritual ministry is God Himself. The context in which it takes place is our troubles.

The Preparation for Ministry

How does one prepare for the kind of ministry which Paul describes? The obvious answer from the text is by learning to let God comfort us by His Spirit in all our troubles. Where does one learn this—college, seminary, Sunday school? It is not conferred by a degree or a diploma; it is learned in the school of faith and obedience.

Let's face it. There are many Christians who are loaded with troubles of every kind and yet do not seem to be equipped to minister to others. It is not just having troubles that equips us for ministry but rather how we respond to them.

The first is a faith issue. Do I believe that God has provided such a gift for me? What is my attitude when trouble comes? Do I yell and scream to God and then expend my own resources trying every kind of human manipulation to get myself out of trouble? It is possible that believing people can pass through many tribulations and never look to the Holy Spirit, whom our Lord promised, as the Source for comfort. They may come out the other side of the troubled time and be no different.

Training for ministry involves submitting to God in our troubles. It is believing in God's goodness and seeing troubles as tools that our Father will use to work His good purposes in us, including conforming us to the image of His Son. A key New Testament idea is that God uses trials to work endurance in us. Someone has defined endurance as the divine alchemy by which trouble is turned into spiritual character. If troubles can be the raw material for heavenly character, then the good news is that in this world we have an unlimited supply.

George MacDonald wrote, "The Son of Man suffered unto death, not that men might not suffer, but that their suffering might be like His."[1] Are you specifically trusting God for the *Paraclete* to come and comfort you in your trouble? Are you submitting to God in your difficulty so that He can use it for your maturity? If so, God is preparing you to be a powerful minister in the lives of hurting people.

There is another facet to this training. Notice 1:5: "For just as the sufferings of Christ flow over into our lives, so also through Christ our comfort overflows."

Now Paul speaks of Christ's sufferings. They flow over into our lives. Is Christ suffering now? He did suffer for us on the cross. We know that work is completed. It is a finished work of redemption. There is no more that needs to be done to provide for our salvation. Does He still suffer?

Christ is seated at the Father's right hand but His body is still in the world. Wherever believers suffer, Christ suffers. Paul commented in Colossians 1:24, "Now I rejoice in what was suffered for you, and I fill up in my flesh what is still lacking in regard to Christ's afflictions, for the sake of his body, which is the church." Paul's attitude was that Christ is still suffering in the world (through His body, the church) and he wanted to share in the suffering.

There are broken people all around us. We can either build a wall around ourselves to block out the pain and ignore it if we can, or we can identify with it and trust God to make us a healing agent in a broken world. Ministry belongs to those who follow Christ in making room in their lives for people. It is part of the preparation for ministry.

The Price of Ministry

"We do not want you to be uninformed, brothers, about the hardships we suffered in the province of Asia. We were under great pressure, far beyond our ability to endure, so that we despaired even of life. Indeed, in our hearts we felt the sentence of death. But this happened that we might not rely on ourselves but on God, who raises the dead" (2 Corinthians 1:8–9).

Ministry is about God comforting us in our troubles so that we can be a comfort to any who are in trouble. Is there a price tag on being a channel of such blessing? There is, and Paul alludes to it in the text quoted above. He refers to a traumatic experience encountered during his ministry in Asia Minor. Was it the riot in Ephesus or being stoned and left for dead in Derbe? We don't know, but whatever it was it took him to the end of his resources. He despaired of life.

God used the experience, says Paul, to destroy his confidence in the flesh and to bring him to childlike dependence upon God. Those drink most deeply of God's comfort who are brought to the end of human resource. Paul had nothing left but the God who raises the dead. He now had something of great substance to share with hurting people, but it was costly. This is the first glimpse of a principle which Paul weaves throughout this epistle. It is illuminated by his allowing us to view the inner recesses of his heart. The principle is, we minister out of our weakness rather than out of our strength.

Remember that this letter was addressed to a local church that was being brutally critical of the apostle. The natural inclination would have been to come on strong. The best defense is a strong offense, we are told. Paul did just the opposite. He allowed them to see his weakness, a man who had no other resource but the God who raises the dead.

If God meets us in our troubles so that we may be a comfort to others who are in trouble, doesn't it follow that the way the message must come through is for us to allow others to see the places in our lives where we have no other resource but God? This idea, of course, not only contradicts fallen human nature but flies in the face of our culture, which says: *Hide your weakness! Put your best foot forward! Come on strong!*

The truth is that showing people our strengths may impress them and up our rating as an effective servant of God, but what communicates the grace of God is for people to see that God has met us in our weakness. It is in our inadequacies that Jesus can best be seen as the One who is enough.

True Ministry Flows from Experience

When celebrities (we no longer have heroes in our society) come to saving faith we are quick to push them into the limelight. I wonder if one of the reasons that Charles Colson is such an effective vessel of God's grace is that the first months of his life as a believer were spent in prison where the evangelical promoters couldn't do him in. We probably find solace for our sagging self-image as Christians to know that some famous individual is a believer. Not only does the limelight make it difficult for such new believers to grow, but it misses the whole idea of ministry. I am not a sports legend, a movie star or a singing sensation—their testimony that God helps them be a success has little to say to me.

I remember a businessman who spoke at a men's fellowship breakfast. His opening line went something like this. "I have started and owned five different business ventures. Four of them have failed and the fifth one is struggling. Let me tell you how God has met me in midst of failure." That man had my undivided attention and the Spirit of God brought help to my heart that morning.

There are areas in all of our lives where we have no answers but the God who raises the dead. He is able to put together our broken dreams, raise our dead hopes from the grave and restore joy in the midst of grief. It is out of this story that true ministry flows.

Let me tell you part of my story which may put Paul's message in shoe leather. My parents were new believers when they married. God granted them three sons of which I am the second. Though I was nine years of age when I publicly declared my faith in Christ, the conscious awareness of God's hand upon my life came much earlier and with it a sense of God's calling to pastoral ministry. There was never a question of being or doing anything else.

Being a classic introvert brought tensions early on. My father was extremely quiet and reserved. My sanguine mother found it difficult to cope with his lack of verbal expression and there was frequent conflict between them; it angered her that my father just didn't talk enough. Friends frequently commented that I was just like my father. So the message was clear, I was quiet and reserved and that was not a good way to be. This became a tension in life as I began to get serious about preparing for pastoral ministry.

My older brother Don is the extrovert. He developed his people skills early and was always at the center of the action. He preceded me to college and by the time I arrived there he was president of the student body. I loved him and admired him but I couldn't miss the comparison. The way he was, I reasoned, is what I needed to be if I was going to make it as a pastor.

By the end of my second year, the pressure was closing in on me. Slipping grades, a failed love relationship that left me feeling inadequate and self-doubt about the ministry were all factors in a downward spiral that ended in depression. That summer found me in a spiritual crisis that brought me to brokenness before God. I remember telling God as I walked the floor in the middle of the night that I didn't need to be a pastor or anything else. If I could just know that I pleased Him, that was enough. I didn't feel there was much to give but what I had was totally yielded to God as best I knew how. Abandonment to God is painful but life-changing. I returned to college a new person. I didn't understand then that God ministers through our weaknesses but somehow I began to believe that God could use an introvert like me.

When I graduated, my brother was in southern California pastoring a growing congregation. He wrote to encourage me to come out west. He was sure he could help find just the right place. It would be good, he thought, for us to be in the same district. For obvious reasons I was more comfortable to stay in the midwest, which I chose to do.

Don was disappointed each time we moved and chose not to head west. During a late night visit in our home in Minneapolis he expressed his longing that he and I might live close someday. He wondered, he said, if I wasn't purposely avoiding him. For the first time I told him of how I had lived in his shadow, had made comparisons, had felt I needed to be like him in order to be successful and how I had finally come with great struggle to accept who God wanted me to be.

He wept in unbelief as he told of growing up with feelings of inferiority because I made better grades in school or was chosen first for the ball team. It was tough trying to stay ahead, he said. That nocturnal conversation was a life-changing moment for both of us. Out of this was born a new relationship. We have never lived closer than 2,000 miles away but we are intimate friends. We send a one-hour cassette tape back and forth about twice a month on which we share our lives and encourage each other in ministry.

Here's the picture: two men, blood brothers, brothers in Christ, both ministers of the gospel but having little or no ministry to one another—all because we had spent our lives competing and comparing. Since that night in Minneapolis, Don has been a minister of God's grace in my life. I can draw upon his strengths because I can see Jesus in his weaknesses.

Your life can be a ministry. It is that for which Christ has called you. Will you follow?

Endnotes

1. George McDonald, *Unspoken Sermons,* First Series, quoted in C.S. Lewis, *The Problem of Pain* (New York: MacMillian, 1962), p. 7.

CHAPTER 1

Christ Is God's Great "Yes"

2 Corinthians 1

Among life's greatest fulfillments is the realization that God's Spirit is working in your life so that His life is being communicated to others in ways that affect spiritual growth. That is the essence of ministry as Paul described it in his second letter to the Corinthian believers. The happy news of this letter is that every believer is called by God to be a minister. In what may be the most personal of all his New Testament letters, the apostle bares his heart about his own ministry so that we might be mentored by a man who learned the deep lessons of servanthood.

Ministry does have a price tag. We have already observed that true ministry involves learning to take God's comfort to meet us in our difficulties and then allowing God to use our weaknesses as a showcase for Christ's fullness. There is a cost to being God's channel of grace.

Another cost involved in ministry has to do with our motives. As we sense God working in us and through us we will both be confronted with the issue of our motives and also the way other people view our motives.

I recall a conversation I had with a young university instructor. His spiritual journey had led him to the place of confronting his motives which in turn had brought conviction about his self-centeredness. In response he was endeavoring to go out of his way to be helpful to others. However, as he evaluated this process he realized that his effort to help others was largely motivated by a desire to win favor and therefore at its root was the same self-centeredness. He was frustrated that every attempt to love others invariably ended in a vicious circle of self-interest.

My heart was drawn to this young man. He was asking the right questions and I felt confident that his searching would ultimately bring him to the gospel. How much better his condition than people who are blind to the fallen state of Adam's race and who go merrily on in their "do-goodism," unaware that their efforts at good works might well flow from the most selfish motives and could just as likely prove a hindrance to God's purposes.

We who are acquainted with Jeremiah's diagnosis of the deceitfulness of the human heart (Jeremiah 17:9) have reason to give careful thought to what motivates us. In God's eyes, why we do something is of more importance than what we do. While there are some folk who seem oblivious to what drives them, it seems to me there are a good many individuals who are paralyzed by constant doubts about their motives. Those doubts are immensely magnified when other people begin to make judgments on their motives. It is easy to fall prey to the paralysis of analysis.

This being the case, I was somewhat startled to read the statement that the Apostle Paul wrote to the Christians in Corinth (2 Corinthians 1:12) in which he boldly spoke of confidence in his motives. Either this man was utterly naive, or else he had a secret that many of us need to know.

The impact of the statement is accentuated when you understand the circumstances in which it was written. Paul was the founding pastor of the congregation in Corinth. After he moved on in his missionary journeys the church was beset with serious difficulties—moral failures, bitter division and doctrinal errors, to name a few. Paul had written a pastoral letter to the saints calling upon them to repent and correct the irregularities. Though some repented, others chose to turn on Paul even though he was their spiritual father. They criticized, falsely accused and rejected his leadership. One of their tactics was to pick apart his motives.

Verses 15 and 16 refer to a particular circumstance. Paul had longed to make a return visit to Corinth. He had written in a previous letter that he hoped to stop on his way to Jerusalem. However, as he traveled he felt compelled by the Holy Spirit to hasten to Jerusalem and thus was not able to make the stop in Corinth.

This of course was ammunition for the critics. "Paul is vacillating, he is not a man of his word, he says yes and no at the same time." Worse still, they judged that since he could not be trusted to keep his promises, his witness about Christ should not be believed either. Now if that wouldn't discourage you and set you to navel gazing, what would?

In the face of this, Paul showed an amazing confidence, stating that in his dealings with them he had been devoutly sincere. In so many words, he affirmed that there were no hidden actions, no hidden motives and no hidden meanings in his words. What a remarkable claim! It needs to be explored, for uncovering the reasons for Paul's confidence

may well open the way for new liberty in your walk with
God.

A Resounding "Amen"

The people in Corinth had characterized Paul as the kind
of person who makes frivolous promises with fickle intentions and never really commits himself to a firm yes or no.
It was an unfair and unfounded criticism and Paul not only
denied it but reminded the believers that he had lived among
them (18 months) and that they were all acquainted with
his lifestyle. Paul was living out Peter's exhortation to the
early Christians to live with such integrity that false accusations would be seen as foolish (1 Peter 2:12).

Their judgments on Paul's motives and his firm denial
would have simply ended in a stalemate and left Paul a
victim of self-doubt had not our mentor viewed the situation from God's point of view. The issue of Paul's integrity
was grounded in the faithfulness of God: "But as surely as
God is faithful, our message to you is not 'Yes' and 'No.'
For the Son of God, Jesus Christ, who was preached
among you by me and Silas and Timothy, was not 'Yes'
and 'No,' but in him it has always been 'Yes' " (2 Corinthians 1:18–19).

The Corinthians had first heard the gospel when Paul
preached in their city, and he reminded them that the gospel
was not a "yes and no" proposition.

At the center of the message is the God who is utterly
faithful. He is a God who makes covenants and keeps them
for a thousand generations. What is God like? He makes
promises—and then He demonstrates His character by
keeping them. And, says Paul, the gospel proclaims that in
sending His one and only Son, Jesus Christ, God has spoken

an eternal "yes" to all His promises (1:19). Jesus is the "yes" pronounced upon every one of God's promises.

Consider the promises which the Scriptures hold out to Adam's race. Unconditional love: "I have loved you with an everlasting love." Forgiveness and cleansing for the vilest of sinners. Abundant life—yes, eternal life. Power to lift us out of our moral helplessness and failure. If those promises are true then it is certainly proper to call it *good news.*

But why believe it? It does seem too good to be true. Human beings early learn the painful lesson of broken promises. People tend to hedge on their promises when it is to their advantage. Why should we expect God to be different? For Paul the answer to that is Jesus Christ.

The plot of the Bible is fairly simple. God made mankind in His own image to love Him and enjoy Him. Mankind chose to rebel and disobey God and was driven from the garden. This loss included both alienation from God and physical death. There in the garden the Creator promised that He would redeem them and restore paradise and that the redemption would come from the seed of the woman. The focus of mankind's hopes across the centuries has rested in that promise. Love, forgiveness, hope, righteousness, peace—all of these were proclaimed to be found in the coming Savior. That is why the incarnation stands as the pivotal event of history. Christ, Himself, is the "yes" to all of God's promises.

Did God proclaim unconditional love? "This is love: not that we loved God, but that he loved us and sent his Son as an atoning sacrifice for our sins" (1 John 4:10). Forgiveness? "In him we have redemption through his blood, the forgiveness of sins" (Ephesians 1:7a). Life and power? "For if, when we were God's enemies, we were reconciled to him through

the death of his Son, how much more, having been reconciled, shall we be saved through his life!" (Romans 5:10).

The resurrection of Christ from the tomb was the ex-
clamation point of God's revelation. It was and is an incredible "yes." Paul wanted the critics in Corinth to
remember that he had preached a message with no ambivalence. It was a message that promised eternal life and
was sealed in blood by a Man who rose from the grave.

The question evoked by the passage is, how does God's
great "yes" in Christ relate to Paul's need for confidence
about his own motives? So God is faithful, but what about
Paul? Verse 20 is the key: "For no matter how many
promises God has made, they are 'Yes' in Christ. And so
through him the 'Amen' is spoken by us to the glory of
God."

To God's great "yes"in Christ, Paul had said a resounding
"amen."

"Amen" is a powerful word. We tend to use it rather glibly,
viewing it as the proper protocol for ending prayers and
other religious rituals. "Amen" means "so let it be." To say
a genuine "amen" is to respond to God's truth by opening
your heart to all His will and purpose.

Have you said, "amen"—I mean from the depths of your
heart? To God's "yes" in Christ have you made a full
surrender? I fear that many are in spiritual defeat because to
God's "yes" they have said a half-hearted "amen." At the
root of the confusion and ambivalence that plague so many
believers is the matter of unresolved inner conflicts, trying
to serve more than one master (Matthew 6:24), having one's
heart attached to conflicting affections.

Nothing brings fresh air and simplicity to the inner life
like firm, clear commitment. Verses 21 and 22 speak of

Paul's sense of inner settledness: "Now it is God who makes both us and you stand firm in Christ. He anointed us, set his seal of ownership on us, and put his Spirit in our hearts as a deposit, guaranteeing what is to come."

When we respond to God with the "amen" of faith and commitment, God sends His Spirit to live in our hearts. The presence of the Holy Spirit is like a down payment (like buying a home or property), a guarantee that the transaction will be completed. It is a seal, a pledge that God has owned the person and will complete that which He has begun (Philippians 1:6).

The basis for Paul's confidence was the realization that truth had come to live in his heart. Not merely truth as an idea or doctrine or philosophy, but truth as a Person. In Christ the very character of God was being formed in him.

That did not make Paul infallible; he still possessed a sinful nature capable of deceit. But he was no longer a victim of his own subjectivity and preoccupation with self. He now had a reference point to guide him, the implanted character of the eternal God.

A Continuing Lordship

The criticism leveled at Paul regarded his expressed intention to stop in Corinth to visit on his way to Jerusalem. His plans had changed so that he was not able to make the visit, and the charge was that the apostle was a "yes" and "no" person who manipulated people for his own advantage. I need to remind myself often that I never know enough about another person to be able to judge his or her motives. If the heart of mankind is so deceitful that we cannot know our own hearts, how can we be so audacious as to judge someone else's?

I am reminded often of the story about a young man traveling alone on a train with a baby in his arms. As night came the other passengers tried to settle down for a sleep. The baby was restless and the young father was not able to quiet it. He walked the aisle and did all he could but to no avail. The growing irritation of the other passengers was finally expressed as one of them said impatiently, "Why don't you take the child to its mother?" The young father replied, "I would like to but she is in a casket in the baggage car." It was a poignant moment and the irritation began to dissolve. One by one the other passengers volunteered to take a turn caring for the baby. That story helps me to remember that my judgments on others might be very different if I knew what was going on in their hearts.

Among the most painful experiences that have come to me in pastoral ministry are those occasions when individuals or perhaps a group of people have brought criticism that was based on a judgment about my motives. Nothing has quite the potential to undermine whatever sense of confidence a person may have. It can leave you distracted and preoccupied with fruitless self-examination. While I was writing this chapter I received a call concerning a young pastor friend who has been devastated by just such a circumstance. He will recover, but it will take a while. Judging people's motives is destructive.

Paul's willingness to let us view his weakness is certainly good cause for encouragement. Though under attack the apostle was able to speak with quiet confidence. Not only had Paul said a resounding "amen" to God's great "yes" in Christ, but there was an ongoing commitment to Christ's lordship.

Paul assured the people in Corinth that he had not

changed his mind thoughtlessly or for his own advantage. Rather, he reminded them that the person who walks with Christ does not make plans in the same fashion as those of the world. He does not say "yes" or "no" according to the whims of his own preference. Not only are we indwelt by God's Spirit but we are led by the Spirit.

Again, let it be clear that claiming to be led by God's Spirit does not make one infallible. We have all experienced the frustration of being manipulated by someone who has donned a super-spiritual air and claimed a direct word from God. My antennae go up when someone announces that God has told them to tell me the message they are about to give. It occurs to me that if in fact God had spoken a message to them they wouldn't need to mention it. It would be obvious by the wisdom conveyed and the humble, gentle demeanor.

However, we are talking about confidence regarding our own motives. When I am endeavoring to walk moment by moment in yieldedness to God's Spirit, when all my plans are available to be amended by Him, I have reason to take confidence in His leading. The Scriptures are replete with God's stated intention to lead His people. Whether the analogy is King, Father or Shepherd, God clearly assumes responsibility to lead His people.

While it is true that our heavenly Father is interested in every detail of our lives and no detail is too small to bring to Him, we must not make the knowing of God's preference about the minutiae of life the evidence of His leading. He may be leading us most effectively when we are least aware of it. The basic issue in God leading us has to do with our purposes and motives. When our minds are informed by Scriptures about God's purposes for His people and when we cultivate a daily walk which affirms Christ's lordship and crucifies the passions of our selfish nature, we can move with confidence that the Good Shepherd will lead us.

I heard Elisabeth Elliot give a helpful talk on learning to follow divine leadership. Her advice was that first we need to set our hearts to do God's will, then inform our minds with the prayerful reading of Scripture so that we understand God's overall purposes for His own and then do what is at hand.

Paul had a new Lord. He later writes in this letter that his great ambition was to please Him in everything. That didn't make him infallible or free from temptation to do things out of selfish desire but it did open a way to escape the vicious circle of a life driven by fallen human nature.

Paul wrote to the Galatian believers, "So I say, live by the Spirit, and you will not gratify the desires of the sinful nature" (5:16).

A Walk in Obedience

Did you notice that Paul appealed to his conscience in his statement of confidence? "Now this is our boast: Our conscience testifies that we have conducted ourselves in the world, and especially in our relations with you, in the holiness and sincerity that are from God" (2 Corinthians 1:12a).

To walk in fellowship with the indwelling Holy Spirit is to walk in light—a light that exposes the depths of our selfishness. One's conscience becomes alive with a new keenness regarding areas to which we were previously blind. Our conscience is not infallible. It is possible to live by one's conscience and still live completely for self. But as we walk in inner fellowship, the conscience will be enlightened. And if we choose to walk in that light, it will beget the kind of confidence Paul exhibited.

Can you say with Paul, "I have no hidden actions?" There is the story of a man who ran door-to-door in his town crying out: "Flee! All is known." The most unlikely individuals panicked and ran.

"I have no hidden motives." Can you say that? "What my conscience has exposed I have obeyed. I don't fully know my own heart, but what God has exposed I have obeyed. I am sincere as far as I know." Is that your testimony?

"My words have no hidden meanings." Is it true for you? "I do not say one thing and mean another so that I can claim to speak the truth and at the same time avoid it. I speak to reveal, not to cover. What I say is what I mean." Can you say that?

People have no right to judge our motives, but they do. We are fallen people who live in a broken world. Part of being a servant is being realistic about our own fallenness and that of others. Paul's secret is essential to walking with confidence.

I recall sweating with this issue a number of years ago when someone wrote me an anonymous note. Actually it was written on an encouragement card. Like a good many churches we had cards in the pew pockets which were embossed with the words, "encouraging one another." The idea was to facilitate the congregants in sending notes of encouragement to other believers. This note was not a word of encouragement (I wish discouragers would use their own stationery!). Usually I avoid reading anonymous cards, feeling that people who won't sign their name are not dealing with their own motives. This note was a frontal attack on my motives suggesting I was in the ministry on a ego trip seeking to fulfill thwarted boyhood dreams. That was one of the nicer things it said.

Reading the note evoked painful memories of other occasions when judgments on my motives had brought inner turmoil. The same temptations began to surface, but this time there was settledness underneath. I took a good while to allow God to search my heart and then recalled this passage. Paul's secret enabled me to honestly face the criticism, admit my fallibility, but at the same time find a basis for confidence.

Those who risk themselves in ministry will suffer judgment on their motives. Count on it. Let Paul be your mentor and build his secret into your life.

CHAPTER 2

Captured by Christ

2 Corinthians 2

One of the ancient poets made reference to the glory that was Greece and the splendor that was Rome. The Roman empire possessed both wealth and power, and as we might expect, when they did something, they did it up big. And being a militaristic society, those who were successful on the battlefield were properly rewarded.

If a general was particularly masterful in the battle the senate might confer upon him an honor that was called a *triumph*. The triumph entitled the general to a glorious entrance into the imperial capital amid the acclaim of the throngs in the streets, orchestrated much like a ticker-tape parade down New York's Fifth Avenue. The procession would be led by dignitaries, including the senators, followed by trumpeters to call the attention of the throng. Next would come slaves carrying spoils from the battle (when the armies of Titus overran Jerusalem in 70 A.D., the sacred articles of the temple were carried in his procession). And then following in the train of the spoils would come the general, resplendent in his battle regalia and riding in his chariot. Tied to the wheels of his chariot, dragged along through the streets, would be a number of the captives taken in the battle, the more famous the better. Bringing up the rear of the procession would be priests swinging censers of burning incense, as a token of thanks to the gods who had blessed the warriors with victory.

It would appear that this is what the Apostle Paul had in mind when he wrote the triumphant note of thanks which closes chapter 2 of Second Corinthians. This note of thanks celebrates a paradox which is at the heart of spiritual ministry. Remember, we are not talking about professional Christian ministry, but about that ministry of the Holy Spirit in the life of the believer in which the life of the indwelling Christ is poured out through him or her to people in need.

Paul's letter of loving but firm discipline had received mixed reviews in Corinth. Many reacted by attacking Paul's motives and character. This second letter has almost a parental feel to it. Every parent has occasion when he or she longs for the child to understand that the discipline, though painful, has come from a loving heart. That note comes through clearly in the opening verses of chapter 2. Note verse 4: "For I wrote you out of great distress and anguish of heart and with many tears, not to grieve you but to let you know the depth of my love for you."

It is in this context that Paul approaches a painful issue that was addressed in his first letter to the Corinthian believers and which was no doubt part of what occasioned this second letter. A prominent member of the church had been involved in an illicit relationship that was shocking even in the loose and licentious climate of Corinth: he was having an affair with his father's wife. Paul had rebuked the believers not only because they had not disciplined the wrongdoer but were instead feeling pride in their own broad-mindedness at being able to overlook such behavior.

Paul had instructed them to excommunicate the offender as a means of awakening him to his spiritual plight. Apparently it had been effective. Discipline is designed for restoration, not destruction. However, it seems that after the man repented, the church had been slow to forgive and restore.

It was in this context that Paul gave thanks for the believer's triumph in Christ and used the analogy of the Roman triumph to uncover the paradox of Christian ministry.

Life in Christ Is a Triumph

In verse 14 Paul gave thanks to God, "who always leads us in triumphal procession in Christ." If, in fact, Paul had the Roman triumph in mind, then we must consider where we might fit in the procession. Are we the dignitaries whose role is to add class to Christ's victorious celebration? Or perhaps like the trumpeters, we are heralds of Christ to call people's attention to the victor. Could we be the slaves, the servants who carry the spoils so as to give public testimony to the glory of the conqueror? Is that what Paul had in mind?

When we read the whole paragraph with the analogy of the Roman triumph in mind, it seems clear that Paul saw himself as a captive, tethered to the chariot wheels and dragged along in Christ's triumphal procession.

It is a startling idea at first. Was Paul engaging in hyperbole? I think not. He was speaking honestly of his own spiritual journey. And here is the paradox of life in Christ.

Paul had never known liberty until he had been captured and enslaved by Christ. He found true freedom in being a bondslave of Jesus. His life became a triumph when he was conquered.

Paul characterized his past life as being a Pharisee of the Pharisees. In the eyes of his peers he was the paragon of virtue. His disciplined life and self-sufficiency made him a force to be reckoned with in the Jewish world. Admired and revered, those looking on from the outside would judge him a man who had it all together. The truth is that Paul was in bondage. There is no joy in self-righteousness. Smug superiority perhaps, or temporary feelings of self-satisfaction, but this is no freedom. Life becomes a constant drivenness, a perpetual struggle to meet an elusive standard always beyond reach. Such was the inner experience of Paul.

Then one day on the road to Damascus Paul met the crucified and risen Christ. The love of Calvary began to melt that cold, proud heart. When Paul heard the call of Jesus, whom he was persecuting, and realized that he was chosen of God, and that the choosing had nothing to do with his own righteousness but was a gift of grace, his self-righteousness was shattered and destroyed. Broken and defenseless, the would-be persecutor held out his hands to be chained to a new master.

The root problem of our race and of every individual is an awesome pride, an inner rebellion against God. That rebellion leads always to one kind of bondage or another, either a slavish captivity to one's own passions or a servitude to the expectations of others. Strangely enough, a man never finds freedom until he is conquered—conquered and captivated by Christ.

Make me a captive, Lord, and then I shall be free;
Force me to render up my sword, and I shall con-
   queror be.
I sink in life's alarms, when by myself I stand;
Imprison me within Thine arms, and strong shall
   be my stand.

George Matheson

Jesus said, "Blessed are the meek, for they will inherit the earth" (Matthew 5:5). The Christian walks in triumph in the procession of the risen Lord, but he walks as a captive, conquered and broken by the love of his crucified Lord.

Do you see it clearly? Paul had been living by a lofty ethic, far higher than most people who call themselves Christians today. But this highly ethical man was killing Christians. Do we understand that one can endeavor to live by the Christian ethic, but if driven by a proud heart and unbroken will, can twist that ethic and justify evil in the name of right?

The believer is not someone who merely endeavors to live by the Christian ethic, but someone whose heart has been captured and whose will has been broken by the love of the crucified Lord.

Life in Christ Is a Testimony

In verse 14 where Paul speaks of God always leading us in triumphal procession in Christ, he adds, "and through us spreads everywhere the fragrance of the knowledge of him." Being led in Christ's triumphal procession spreads *His* fragrance.

The Roman general who rode into the imperial city in triumph, dragging his captives behind him, received the tumultuous cheers of the throng. The cheers were for the general, not the captives, but in a sense the captives were the cause of the applause. The captives were the evidence, the testimony of victory.

Our lives, says Paul, are to be the testimony of Christ's triumph. The captive has nothing to exhibit but his own broken weapons. In the Roman triumphs the captives were often compelled to carry their broken spears, twisted swords or the armor that had been pierced.

Paul's testimony of Christ's triumph was his own broken weapons of self-righteousness. He told the Philippian believers of his weapons: "a Hebrew of Hebrews; in regard to the law, a Pharisee; . . . as for legalistic righteousness, faultless" (3:5b–6). Then he proceeded to tell them that all of it was loss for the sake of Christ. He considered it rubbish that he might gain Christ.

In Romans 7 Paul confessed the poverty of his inner life. The things I want to do, I cannot do, and those I do not want to do, I end up doing, was his confession. His weapons were useless in the battlefield of the soul. Paul's confession ended with a cry of despair—"Who will rescue me from this body of death?" (7:24b)—but despair was immediately transformed into a cry of joy because of Christ's victory.

The proud Pharisee bowed his knee one day and received grace, a free gift from the nail-pierced hand of the Savior. He wrote to the Galatians, "May I never boast except in the cross of our Lord Jesus Christ, through which the world has been crucified to me, and I to the world" (6:14).

I recall attending a Youth for Christ directors' conference when I was in college. I was directing a small rally in our college town and the school paid my way to attend the conference. I was a bit overwhelmed when I entered the hotel ballroom filled with cholerics and sanguines. Personalities were being circulated and success stories highlighted. I sought shelter by the far wall and took a spectator stance. In a moment I sensed someone standing beside me and was surprised to see that it was Dr. Bob Cook, who was at that time president of YFC. As he introduced himself, though I knew who he was, I immediately sensed that he understood what I was feeling.

"Paul," he said, "there are a lot of powerful people here; I wonder what guys like you and me should do." He had won my heart. There was a fragrance about him. His whole approach to people was marked by a difference. I didn't know what it was then, but now I understand that it was grace, not social grace, but God's grace. In his hands he had broken weapons, having been conquered and captivated by Christ. It was evident he had nothing to defend and nothing of self to promote. I was immediately drawn to the Lord who had won him. I can still smell the fragrance.

When the weapons of self-righteousness, self-promotion and self-glory are broken and made useless, the life in Christ bears a fragrant testimony to the completeness of Christ's victory.

Life in Christ Involves Tension

The fragrance of Christ's victory is not a universal blessing. It is in fact a source of tension. In verses 15 and 16, Paul further commented on the fragrance: "For we are to God the aroma of Christ among those who are being saved and those who are perishing. To the one we are the smell of death; to the other, the fragrance of life. And who is equal to such a task?"

To the person seeking for spiritual life and reality, the fragrance of Christ in a man or woman will be like a fresh ocean breeze bringing life and renewal. Like Paul they are weary of the bondage of the self-life and constant inner defeat, ready to humble their proud heart and bend the knee. For them being captured by Christ holds the hope of true liberty.

But, says Paul, to that individual consumed by the pride and rebellion of a hardened heart, and somehow blind to their bondage, the fragrance of Christ's captives are like the stench of death. Every contact with believers is a fresh reminder of the unsettled, inner conflicts that rage in the heart.

Do you echo Paul's heart cry? "And who is equal to such a task?" In the closing verses of chapter 2 Paul affirms his commitment to integrity in ministry: "We do not peddle the word of God for profit. On the contrary, in Christ we speak before God with sincerity, like men sent from God" (2:17).

There are those who talk religion but who do not care enough to take risks and deal with true spiritual issues.

That was the problem in Corinth. A member of the church was having sexual relations with his father's wife. At first, the church avoided the issue and took subtle pride in their broad-mindedness. It takes courage and commitment to lovingly confront.

Does it help to excommunicate such a man? Have you considered that when a person is struggling in mortal combat with something that is destroying his soul, if his closest friends act as if nothing is wrong but just smile and go their way, they make it a hundred times more difficult to escape? I am convinced that often people involved in immoral situations are inwardly crying out for someone to care enough to confront and demand change, but friends smile and look past them and in so doing condemn them to their bondage.

Paul's letter of correction awakened the believers to their obligation of love and they called the man to account. This led to the severe measure of excommunication. Paul's concern in this second letter was that the man had repented but was not being forgiven and welcomed back to fellowship. The apostle feared that the erring brother would be destroyed instead of restored, thus playing into the hands of the enemy.

Church folk these days have little stomach for church discipline. The situation in Corinth is played out again and again in our congregations and few find the courage to act in love. Those who flounder in sin are most often either condemned or ignored and left to the devices of the tempter.

This whole area is so very difficult, you say. Paul would readily agree. It seems to me that what he is saying in this passage which portrays the paradox of life in Christ, is that we cannot minister to others in trouble (particularly to those in moral trouble) unless we come as someone who has been conquered and captured by Christ. When we come bearing in our hands the broken weapons of our own self-righteousness, the fragrance of God's grace will be an aroma of hope. Only then are we equipped for the ministry of discipline and restoration.

The number of evangelical leaders who have experienced moral failures is making a clear statement about the shallowness that seems to characterize much of our activity. An even greater evidence about the superficial nature of our commitment is our inability to exercise both loving discipline and restoration.

It doesn't take much spiritual maturity to overlook the

moral failures of fellow believers and act as if nothing is happening. You can call it love and compassion if you wish, but the truth is that it likely represents neglect and cowardice.

It doesn't take much spiritual stature to condemn the fallen one from a distance and write them off. One can easily mistake self-righteous disdain for holy anger.

Paul's challenge to the Galatians was: "Brothers, if someone is caught in a sin, you who are spiritual should restore him gently" (6:1).

Paul indicated that the ministry of restoration requires spiritual stature. It is for those who have been conquered by Christ and whose weapons of self-righteousness have been broken.

> My heart is weak and poor until its master finds;
> It has no spring of action sure, it varies with the
>   wind;
> It cannot freely move till thou hast wrought its
>   chain;
> Enslave it with Thy matchless love, and deathless it
>   shall reign.
>
> George Matheson

CHAPTER 3

Life in the Spirit

2 Corinthians 3

Primary to God's concern for each of us is our heart attitude. Jesus taught that man's basic problem is the condition of the heart.

> What comes out of a man is what makes him "unclean." For from within, out of men's hearts, come evil thoughts, sexual immorality, theft, murder, adultery, greed, malice, deceit, lewdness, envy, slander, arrogance and folly. (Mark 7:20–22)

Jesus, of course, was not speaking of the physical organ that pumps the blood, but of the innermost part of our being, the seat of the affections and will. In all of His dealings with us, God seeks to redeem us by bringing a change of heart. And because the heart is the throne of our lives, and because we are rebels at heart, there is a perverseness within us that will always prefer a religion that deals only with the externals.

The law which God gave ancient Israel at Sinai was given

to reveal the character of God, to regulate their relationship to him and, by revealing the moral bankruptcy of their hearts, drive them to seek divine mercy and forgiveness. Like Adam's children have always done, they were prone to miss the spiritual dimension of God's commands.

When a lawyer asked Jesus to identify the greatest command, his answer revealed the heart issue: "Love the Lord your God with all your heart and with all your soul and with all your mind and with all your strength" (12:30).

The ministry of the Apostle Paul was dogged by the Judaizers wherever he went. These Jewish teachers preached a righteousness based on external conformity to Jewish law and custom. Paul, the Pharisee-turned-gospel-preacher, evoked volatile reactions and sometimes riots. In Corinth Paul was hauled into court and Sosthenes, the ruler of the synagogue, suffered a beating at the hands of the angry mob.

While questions about the law were not the major issue at Corinth as they were in Galatia, there was a tension that only added to the criticism being leveled at Paul. His firm but loving letter of correction had brought rejection and criticism. In this second letter Paul wrote from the heart, hoping that their understanding of his ministry might make for reconciliation. His openness gives us further insight into the nature of spiritual ministry.

A Letter Written on the Heart

Being open with people is always a risk. When people are misinterpreting your motives, being open only gives them more ammunition. This is, no doubt, one of a number of reasons that we tend to choose self-preservation tactics. Larry Crabb says that the tendency to self-preservation is one of the most destructive things present in the life of the church.[1] When a Christian brother sins we are afraid to risk loving confrontation and instead choose to stay within our comfort zone. The choice to preserve rather than to risk is what destroys the hope of true community.

Paul could hear the critics in Corinth saying that his letter was only an attempt to justify himself or to beg commendation from the believers there. His comments in chapter 3 of Second Corinthians serve to dispel such criticism by the surprise tactic of drawing a new frame of reference. You, he says of the believers in Corinth, are the only letter of recommendation that I need.

Notice the comments about the believers being a letter:

1. "You yourselves are our letter, written on our hearts, known and read by everybody" (3:2). They were held in deep affection by Paul and he spoke of them with pride and joy wherever he went. I have an idea that they were surprised to hear that.

2. "You . . . are a letter from Christ, the result of our ministry" (3:3a). Paul had preached the good news of righteousness by faith in the saving work of Christ. There in the cosmopolitan city of Corinth, eaten through with licentiousness and corruption, Christ had brought His church to birth. It was God's mighty work, but Paul understood that he was a vessel in God's hand. They were a letter written by Christ but also a letter about the validity of Paul's ministry.

3. They were a letter "written not with ink but with the Spirit of the living God, not on tablets of stone,

but on tablets of human hearts" (3:3b). Christian ministry is a religion of the heart. Its goal is not to produce people whose behavior is shaped by legal strictures, but rather men and women revolutionized in the heart by the mighty work of God's Spirit.

Paul was quick to point out that while the spiritual realities present in the church in Corinth gave him confidence about the validity of his ministry, he did not claim any competence in himself. However, he was not embarrassed to affirm that by God's power he was made a competent minister of a new covenant. The reference to the new covenant draws the line between the preaching of the law and the saving gospel of Christ: "Not of the letter but of the Spirit; for the letter kills, but the Spirit gives life" (3:6).

The Letter That Kills

It is difficult for many people to grasp the fact that there is a preaching that kills. The church was easily deceived by it in the first century, and discernment is in woefully short supply these days. Preachers of the law sound so biblical and appear so religious and proper that God's people are prone to be blinded to the danger. Preaching that calls only for external obedience kills. Do we understand that? How does such preaching kill?

> 1. It kills by producing hypocrisy. In particular danger are those who have been raised in a some-what disciplined lifestyle. Their ability to conform their external behavior to some semblance of righteous living easily blinds them to the awful

realities of a wicked heart. Jeremiah 17:9 warns that the heart of man is desperately wicked and deceitful above all things. These dear folk go blindly on unaware that their "good works" may be motivated by selfish pride or for personal gain or even to take advantage of others. Comparing themselves with others who are less disciplined or lack social graces brings feelings of smug self-satisfaction. The longer one is deceived by pride the more it kills any hope for change.

2. Preaching that addresses only external behavior also kills by producing despair and bondage. People who are not well disciplined in their lifestyle or who do not feel that they compare favorably with others will find such preaching a cause for despair. Repeated failures in attempts to bring one's behavior in line with the ideal only drives one further down into the slough of despondency. Though such people may have periods in their life when they do fairly well, it is never enough. The conscience is never at peace. Their refusal to be a hypocrite only condemns them to bondage. Inner conflict is a constant companion.

In his book *The Meaning of Persons*, Paul Tournier uses a helpful analogy as he writes of the *person* and the *personage*. The person, he says, is the reality of the inner life. It has to do with character, integrity, motivation and desires. The personage, on the other hand, is the external behavior pattern which may be shaped by parental demand, peer pressure or religious conformity. His observation is that the greater the incongruity between the person and the personage, the greater the possibility of mental and emotional illness.

Spiritual wholeness comes when the personage, the outer behavior pattern, is a true expression of the inner heart. A person cannot dare to live out the inner passions of the human heart unless there has come a power that can cleanse the wellsprings of the soul. Adam and Eve hid in the garden. They hid from God, from one another and from themselves. When the inner realities of our lives are incongruent with our lifestyle and image, life is a bondage lived in constant fear of exposure. It is a game of hide and seek. But there is a way to liberty.

Liberty in the Spirit

My observation is that there are not as many gospel preachers as we might think. I belong to a denomination whose doctrine is Christ-centered, committed to the authority of the Scriptures and evangelical. I don't know of any pastors in our fellowship who do not believe the gospel, but I am not sure that we are all gospel preachers.

We can preach from the Bible and yet do little more than moralize. We can hold up God's standards and call people to do better and try harder. The Scriptures hold a wealth of insight about human nature and the moral universe that we can use to counsel people toward "successful" living. Such teaching can be done in the flesh, motivated by human effort and pride. In the end it leaves the heart unchanged and it is not life-giving.

Paul declared himself a competent minister of the new covenant. He spoke in confidence that just as God had made him competent so He would do the same for the Corinthian believers. In this study we have defined ministry as the life of God at work in my life in such a way as to bring growth and spiritual fruit in the lives of others. God intends for every believer to be a life-giving minister. What a privilege!

The new covenant of which Paul spoke was foreseen by the prophets. Ezekiel spoke of it:

> I will give you a new heart and put a new spirit in you; I will remove from you your heart of stone and give you a heart of flesh. And I will put my Spirit in you and move you to follow my decrees and be careful to keep my laws. (36:26–27)

Here is the hope for liberty—a change from within, a heart given to obedience empowered by God's Spirit. This is the covenant made possible by the death of Christ in our place and by His mighty resurrection. This is the glorious reality that God calls us to live out and communicate.

Notice how Paul speaks of the glory as he compares the old covenant and the new. The old covenant of the Mosaic law had its glory:

> Now if the ministry that brought death, which was engraved in letters on stone, came with glory, so that the Israelites could not look steadily at the face of Moses because of its glory, fading though it was, will not the ministry of the Spirit be even more glorious? If the ministry that condemns men is glorious, how much more glorious is the ministry that brings righteousness! For what was glorious has no glory now in comparison with the surpassing glory. And if what was fading away came with glory, how much greater is the glory of that which lasts! (2 Corinthians 3:7–11)

The law is a schoolmaster, says Paul in Galatians, to lead us to Christ. When it is preached without pointing to Christ it kills. Yet this law engraved in stone had a glory. When Moses came down from Mount Sinai with the tablets of stone his face was ablaze with the glory of God. The Israelites could not gaze steadily upon him until the glory faded, for it was a fading glory.

Moses wore a veil over his face so his countrymen could not see that fading glory. Paul alludes to that veil as being symbolic of the spiritual veil that still covers the minds of Jewish people so that when they read the old covenant it does not point them to Christ (3:13–15).

The new covenant, in contrast, is life-giving and has a surpassing glory, a glory that lasts. This glory has to do with righteousness. It does not merely call for righteous performance but rather offers a new heart and a righteousness that changes the believer from the inside out. The new birth brings the indwelling Holy Spirit who empowers the believer to obey. Paul says in verse 17, "Now the Lord is the Spirit, and where the Spirit of the Lord is, there is freedom."

Think about your ministry. Is it life-giving? Are you a person who gives Bible talks to helpless, struggling seekers telling them to do better and try harder? Such a ministry kills and imprisons. Or are you announcing hope for a changed heart and the inner power to live with integrity? Your neighbors do not need more external expectations heaped upon them. They are already overwhelmed with the expectations of their boss, their spouse or their mother-in-law—not to mention their own expectations. They need to glimpse the glory.

We are ministers of a new covenant. This ministry has a glory that surpasses the Old Testament law. The glory is glimpsed in the life of the messenger. There is a message to be spoken but the credibility of it grows from the glory that shines in the countenance of the believer. Paul concludes chapter 3: "And we, who with unveiled faces all reflect the Lord's glory, are being transformed into his likeness with ever-increasing glory, which comes from the Lord, who is the Spirit" (3:18).

Notice the elements present in this life-giving ministry:

1. The minister has an unveiled face. There is an openness and vulnerability that allow the inner realities to shine. In verse 12 Paul says that "since we have such a hope, we are very bold." The issue is not that I have something to show but rather that Christ lives in me and He is worthy to be seen. Self-consciousness and concern for my own glory will lower the veil.

2. The minister's countenance reflects the Lord's glory. When I look into the mirror in the morning I don't notice a bright light shining from my face. But if I am cultivating the inner life and learning to gaze with the eye of faith into the face of Jesus Christ, I can have confidence that something of the Lord's glory will shine through to seeking pilgrims.

3. Ministers of the new covenant are being transformed into the likeness of Christ with ever-increasing glory. The glory that shines out is working powerfully within to transform the character and heart. Do you see the integrity we spoke of earlier? The glory that is seen on the face reflects an inner

reality being wrought by the power of God.

4. The glory that transforms is not a power that we possess but rather a Person who possesses us. Dr. A.B. Simpson wrote a poem that sings this truth in the believer's heart. Part of it reads:

Once it was my working, His it hence shall be;
Once I tried to use Him, Now He uses me;
Once the power I wanted, Now the mighty One;
Once for self I labored, Now for Him alone.
All in all forever, Jesus will I sing;
Everything in Jesus, and Jesus everything.

The story is told of a vicar in London who was eating his lunch in the vicarage and was looking out the window toward the church. He noticed a large man, dressed in working clothes, who paused in front of the church, looked both ways and then went in. The vicar was curious but decided not to pursue it. However, when he noticed it happen the next day, his curiosity was piqued and on the third day he was hiding in the balcony at noon.

Sure enough, right at noon the door to the sanctuary opened and in walked the hulk of a man. His paw of a hand pulled off his cap as he walked to the front. There he paused at the altar table and looked up toward the cross. The vicar could barely hear the whispered words, "Jesus, this is Jim." The vicar's heart was warmed as he saw Jim come day after day. Then suddenly the visits stopped. It was not until some months later that he learned the rest of the story.

Jim was a truck driver. One day he was involved in a serious accident and taken to the municipal hospital where he was placed in a large ward, inhabited by men from the street. Drunkards, criminals and riff-raff were his fellow patients. It was not a pleasant place for the nurses; one nurse came out of the ward one day in disgust and refused to return, bemoaning the crude language, ribald humor and lack of respect or gratitude.

Over a period of time, however, things began to change. The nurses commented one day that there had in fact been a remarkable change in the atmosphere of the ward. There were expressions of gratitude at times, and downright wholesome laughter. One of the nurses inquired of one of the men what had caused it.

"Ma'am," he said, "you will have to ask Jim; he is in bed number five." Later she stopped at Jim's bed and commented on the change taking place among the men. "Well, Ma'am," Jim responded, "I don't rightly know how to explain this to you. It is just that every day right at noon, Jesus Christ comes walking into this ward and stands at the foot of my bed. And He says, 'Jim, this is Jesus.' "

Jim had cultivated an inner walk with Christ. The overflow was a life-giving ministry which he could not explain. There is ministry that kills, and ministry that sets free. Christ can make us able ministers of the new covenant.

Endnotes

1. Larry Crabb, *Inside Out* (Colorado Springs, CO: NavPress, 1988), pp. 196–197.

CHAPTER 4

The Cost of Communicating

2 Corinthians 4:1–15

One would think that communication would be quite simple these days with all the wonderful instruments we have to transfer information. Radio, television, communication satellites, fax machines, computers and printers that operate at unheard of speeds and printing presses to duplicate thousands of pieces per minute are all in our arsenal of communication tools. Events that happen on any continent of earth can be broadcast into the living rooms of our nation moments later.

Yet strangely enough, with all these marvelous tools of instant communication, the world is still beset with vast problems that stem from our inability to understand one another. Torrents of words flow between us, but the chasms that separate us seem to grow wider.

A woman tells me that after several years of marriage she still doesn't really know her husband. She filled in the blanks of her statement by adding that she didn't know who he voted for in the last election, or even the football team he rooted for last weekend.

It is not a mystery. A bit of reflection should make us realize that while the electronic wonders can put us in instant contact with one another, the real problems of communication are in a different dimension. The gadgets can bridge the gaps of time and space and even language to some degree, but the real obstacles are pride, prejudice, fear, hatred and moral blindness. These are the issues that remain to be addressed. The cost of long distance calls continues to come down, but real communication is still costly.

At the center of the Christian proclamation is the ultimate act of costly communication. We call it the incarnation. The infinite, eternal Creator took on human flesh to live among us.

I have celebrated 56 Advent seasons (I am not counting the first three, since it was not until my third birthday that I fully grasped the dimensions of the incarnation) and while each one leaves me in increasing awe and wonder, I am aware that we cannot begin to fathom the cost involved in God's enfleshment, nor the fullness of the grace that is offered.

In the second Corinthian letter, the Apostle Paul opened his heart so the believers he had left behind in that city could understand the nature of God's call upon his life. His first letter of firm and loving discipline had drawn severe criticism and rejection from a vocal group in the church there, and rather than confronting the critics, Paul hoped that baring his heart might disarm them and open the door for healing. His transparency has afforded the saints of succeeding generations insight into the nature of spiritual ministry.

Remember, when we use the word "ministry" we are not speaking of professional ministry, as in clergy, but rather the powerful work of the Holy Spirit in the life of every believer by which the life and fullness of the indwelling Christ is mediated to other people so that their lives are touched spiritually. If you are a believer, God has called you to ministry. Your life can be a fountain of refreshment to needy people. Paul is describing God's work in his life.

The fourth chapter of Second Corinthians speaks to the issue of communication. As we saw in chapter 1, the God of all comfort comforts us in all our troubles so that we may be a comfort to any who are in difficulty. That is at the core of ministry. How is the reality of God's powerful comfort in our troubles communicated to other hurting people? Is communication easy? No, we have seen that it is difficult and quite costly.

The key text in the chapter puts the wonder of the incarnation at the center of ministry: "For God, who said, 'Let light shine out of darkness,' made his light shine in our hearts to give us the light of the knowledge of the glory of God in the face of Christ" (4:6).

The same infinite Creator who caused light to fill the physical universe, has shined in the darkness of the spiritual universe. John declared that Jesus is that light: "The Word became flesh and made his dwelling among us. We have seen his glory, the glory of the One and Only, who came from the Father, full of grace and truth" (John 1:14).

It is at the new birth, says Paul, that this light of revelation shines in the heart of the believer. One of the evidences of the new birth is spiritual sight. We are able to see the light of the knowledge of the glory of God in the face of Jesus Christ. Like the blind man Jesus healed, we cannot explain it but we testify that "I was blind but now I see!" (9:25).

If the incarnation was the costliest communication that

has ever taken place, then we should not be surprised that our involvement in the ongoing enfleshment of truth should be costly as well.

The Call to Costly Integrity

> Therefore, since through God's mercy we have this ministry, we do not lose heart. Rather, we have renounced secret and shameful ways; we do not use deception, nor do we distort the word of God. On the contrary, by setting forth the truth plainly we commend ourselves to every man's conscience in the sight of God. (2 Corinthians 4:1–2)

Here is a powerful appeal to integrity. The person who is going to follow Christ and witness of His life within must first stand with a clear conscience before God, and then stand before others as an open book with nothing to hide.

In the last chapter we talked about spiritual liberty. It grows out of inner wholeness in which the realities of the soul are congruent with the outward profession. There is confidence and freedom when our lifestyle is flowing naturally out of inner spiritual realities. What liberty when there is nothing to hide! I am on the inside what I appear to be on the outside. We have all experienced the discomfort of witnessing; often the fear comes because we are merely talking about a religious doctrine or belief, rather than witnessing to an inner reality. We would like for our neighbor to see Christ and know how it ought to be, but we would rather he didn't see how it really is inside of us.

Paul wrote to the Corinthians that he had renounced secret and shameful ways. He had been away from them for awhile. They had been barraged by distorted reports from his critics. He wanted them to remember that his life had been an open book when he lived among them.

Being an authentic person does not require the pouring out of one's guts and the continual rehearsing of one's troubles. It does involve congruity of the outer person with the inner heart. The authentic believer has made the moral decision to renounce secret and shameful ways and to adopt the daily discipline of endeavoring to speak the truth. This involves, says Paul, teaching the Scriptures plainly and avoiding the temptation to take the edge off truth so as to justify one's own shortcomings. If the Word of God does not have a cutting edge in our own lives, we cannot expect that our witness will carry authority in the lives of skeptical seekers. Communication is costly.

Home Bible studies have become a powerful means of witness and growth for millions of pilgrims. It seems to me that the secret is twofold. Not only does it give opportunity for unbelievers to be exposed to Scripture in a non-threatening atmosphere, but it allows them to relate to believers in an authentic manner. The unbeliever may respect the high standards of his Christian neighbor and be somewhat impressed with his lifestyle. But it is seeing that the Christian neighbor shares the same human frailties, faces the same fears and frustrations, struggles with the same temptations, yet possesses an inner power that gives a new dimension to life—that makes the Scriptures come alive. It is this witness that can open the unbelieving heart to the Word of God.

I have been aided in my witness by training that has taught me how to verbalize the gospel in a clear and sensitive fashion and how to use conversations to address the ultimate questions in a comfortable way. Such preparation is basic to serious discipleship. But none of it is adequate unless we are willing to pursue the costly discipline of integrity. Integrity in the life of the witness lends authenticity to the message.

The Pain of Communicating with the Blinded

"And even if our gospel is veiled, it is veiled to those who are perishing. The god of this age has blinded the minds of unbelievers, so that they cannot see the light of the gospel of the glory of Christ, who is the image of God" (4:3–4).

Though his second Corinthian letter was conciliatory, Paul faced the charges of the critics head-on. He affirmed that his ministry had been above board, he had lived among them in honesty and openness, and he boldly claimed that he could commend himself to every person's conscience. Such a witness, we should think, would elicit a universally positive response.

Paul introduces a harsh reality into the formula for communicating the good news. The apostle points out that no matter how bright the light is (the glory of God in the face of Jesus Christ), there are many individuals who either cannot or will not see it. The fact is, says Paul, that the god of this world has blinded the minds of unbelievers.

There is a veil over the eyes of the Jewish people (3:15), so that when they read the law they are not able to see the Christ to whom it points (Galatians 3:24). In the same vein, Jesus said to the Pharisees, "You diligently study the Scriptures, because you think that by them you possess eternal life. These are the Scriptures that testify about me, yet you refuse to come to me to have life" (John 5:39–40).

The Pharisees thought that their commitment to the Scriptures would guarantee them eternal life. The fact is their blindness caused them to reject the Son to whom the

Scriptures point and who is the source of eternal life.

There are numerous ways that the enemy of our souls blinds people so that they are not able to see the glory. Religious pride is one of his favorite weapons and very appealing to fallen mankind. Satan's appeal to Eve was that by eating the forbidden fruit she and Adam could be like God. At the root of all sin is pride. Mankind is by nature religious. We are made to know God and enjoy him. But sin has twisted that innate desire so that now we want to be God.

Religion is attractive to Adam's children as long as it does not involve bowing the knee to the sovereign Creator. For many religion is a means of dealing with longings of the human heart, seeking to satisfy the demands of whatever deities exist, and at the same time endeavoring to retain sovereign control over one's own life and destiny. If a savior is needed, we choose to be our own savior no matter how great the cost.

In our evangelism training we interview people on the street about their religious beliefs. The vast majority see themselves as religious and identify themselves as Christians. Yet for most of them Christ is merely a religious figure; by their own admission their faith is in their own righteousness. They can understand the words of the gospel, but their eyes are blinded to the glory of God in Christ.

Intellectual pride is another means our enemy uses to blind people. Out of the Enlightenment has come an awesome confidence in the human intellect. To assume that the mind of man is the highest intelligence in the universe leads to the belief that one's own rationality is the final appeal to truth and authority. It follows that anything outside the limited sphere of man's rationality is unreal and impossible. Seeing oneself as the center of the universe makes the idea of God unnecessary and somewhat offensive.

C.S. Lewis, in the book *The Problem of Pain*, follows this line of reasoning to its absurd conclusion. If the mind of man is the highest intelligence in the universe, then our minds have come into being without a Creator, a result of cause and effect in the processes of nature. It follows then that the mind is only a chemical process having evolved out of inorganic materials. If this be true, then I have no reason to trust my thoughts as being valid. There is no reason to believe that the chemical process going on in my mind and causing these thoughts has any meaning or correlation to reality (if there is such a thing). When I think a profound thought it may only be a chemical reaction from having had too much pepperoni on the pizza. And what reason is there to believe that the thought that there is no God has validity either?[1]

Many cannot see God's glory in Christ because their rational presuppositions rule it out before they have a chance to look. Sin has at its root a fierce pride in which man has lifted his heart in rebellion and denied God His central place in his life. False religion and intellectual pride are attempts to avoid the issue. I am fascinated by people who talk endlessly about the search for truth, but who have no interest in talking with anyone who claims to have found it. Searching for truth appeals to one's sense of pride, but finding the truth demands submitting to it.

You have met, no doubt, people who throw up a smoke screen of unanswerable pseudo-intellectual questions to explain why they do not commit themselves to God. Someone has suggested that if we brought together the top 10 scientists in the world and let a 10-year-old ask them questions, it is likely that they could only answer about a third of the inquiries. Technology operates in a world of largely unanswered questions. We don't have all the answers about the infinite God, but the glory of God can be seen in the face of Jesus Christ.

We are talking about communicating spiritual realities. Paul says that even though the light is bright, some will not see it because they are blinded. How do you communicate with people who will not or cannot see? Paul's point is that there is a painful patience that is called for and an unconditional love which is the unanswerable argument.

Proclaiming Christ, Not Ourselves

> But we have this treasure in jars of clay to show that this all-surpassing power is from God and not from us. We are hard pressed on every side, but not crushed; perplexed, but not in despair; persecuted, but not abandoned; struck down, but not destroyed. We always carry around in our body the death of Jesus, so that the life of Jesus may also be revealed in our body. For we who are alive are always being given over to death for Jesus' sake, so that his life may be revealed in our mortal body. (2 Corinthians 4:7–11)

How do we communicate with people who are blinded by pride? One answer is, humbly. Humility is not self-depreciation, but a realistic view of who God is and who I am. I can talk about proclaiming Christ but what really comes naturally to me is proclaiming myself. Fallen human nature wants to be glorified, to be admired, to be sought after, to be pitied.

God plans for His glory to be manifested in the lives of
His children, but make no mistake about it, the Scripture
is clear that God will not give His glory to another (Isaiah
42:8). At first glance, God's plan makes no sense to us. Paul
says we have this treasure in earthen vessels; translate that
"mud pots." It strikes us as incongruous. Treasure should
be in ornate treasure chests.

No, God's intention is to make it unmistakable to the
observer that the all-surpassing power (the glory) is from
God and not from us. At the time of our 25th wedding
anniversary Jeanie and I visited the jewelry store of a friend
to look at diamonds. I remember well that he took the gems
out of the pouch and placed them on a piece of plain black
cloth. The contrast highlighted the beauty of the diamonds.
The glory of God is best displayed in mud pots. God is not
looking for superstars, just mud pots.

In the mud pot analogy we see the recurring theme of
Second Corinthians: God ministers in our weaknesses, not
our strengths. Paul says that the pain and pressure points of
our lives are stuff out of which true ministry flows:

- We are hard pressed on every side, pressed down by
  heavy weights. But not crushed! The glory is not
  that we escape the crushing pressures that plague the
  human race, but that by the power of Christ we are
  not crushed.
- We are perplexed. Are Christians bewildered and
  perplexed at times? Yes, says Paul. The glory is not
  that believers are never perplexed, but rather that in
  the bewilderment they do not despair.
- We are persecuted. Are believers persecuted? Does
  God allow that? He does. The glory is not that God's

servants are spared persecution, but rather that they are not abandoned. God suffers with them and sustains them.

- We are struck down. Are God's people knocked down? They are knocked down but never knocked out! We lose battles but we are not defeated in the long run. The glory is not that we always win, but rather that we are not destroyed. God preserves His own.

Paul's vivid depiction of the mud pot role is that we always carry around in our body the death of Jesus, so that the life of Jesus may also be revealed in our body.

We started this conversation talking about all the modern communication gadgets that we have in hand to transfer information. Paul has reminded us that the real issues of communication are still difficult and costly. But what a rewarding experience to know that the glory of God is somehow coming through in my life to touch and change the life of another.

I visited this week with a pastor who serves as an adjunct professor at our seminary. He is highly regarded by both faculty and students, and I was anxious to get better acquainted. His face radiates joy, his smile is engaging, his manner disarming. He walks with a noticeable limp. I noticed that he had to snap his knee brace so he could sit down. In the few moments we visited he communicated God's grace to my heart and showed great sensitivity to the pain I am experiencing in my walk.

As he got up to go (snapping his knee brace in place) I inquired as to whether he had ever had polio. Yes, he said, he had polio as a young boy in Malaysia but had made a complete recovery. Seeing the question on my face he offered that his present condition was the result of 13 months of beatings and torture after he became a Christian. He was in almost constant pain, he said, but encouraged me with the reminder that pain does not hinder our effectiveness in ministry but is rather the very stuff out of which it grows. Communication is costly.

Dr. A.B. Simpson spoke to the root issue in his hymn "Not I, But Christ":

> Not I but Christ be honored, loved, exalted;
> Not I but Christ be seen, be known, be heard;
> Not I but Christ in every look and action;
> Not I but Christ in every thought and word.
> Oh, to be saved from myself, dear Lord!
> Oh, to be lost in Thee!
> Oh, that it might be no more I,
> But Christ that lives in me!

Endnotes

1. C.S. Lewis, *The Problem of Pain* (New York: MacMillan, 1962), pp. 14–15.

CHAPTER 5

Faith That Beholds the Unseen

2 Corinthians 4:16–5:10

Wat one human being, since the time of Christ, has made the greatest impact upon Western civilization? I think most of us would think of the Apostle Paul. Not only have his writings greatly influenced the philosophies and institutions of the Western world, but he was the instrument in God's hands used to plant the church in Europe in the midst of the powerful and pagan Roman Empire. In spite of the bitter persecution, he almost single-handedly planted congregations in city after city sowing seeds that would later blossom into a powerful movement.

Perhaps you have wondered, as I have, what made this man tick. I have never suffered outright persecution for my faith, but as I recall, even being written off as a fanatic by a few individuals seemed akin to martyrdom at the time. It is difficult to fathom what would cause a person to suffer what Paul did, and keep going (2 Corinthians 11:24–27). He was highly motivated in his ministry, that is obvious enough. But what drove him?

Fortunately, we don't have to speculate on that question. The New Testament is not a theological treatise that addresses the question of God at arms length; most of it is composed of letters that speak the language of the heart. What better way to explore the inner life of another person than to read his or her mail! We have noted that Paul's second letter to the Corinthian believers contains the most intimate insights into his heart and his ministry.

The subject in chapters 3 and 4 speaks to the very heart of what ministry is about. The glory of God in Christ is revealed in the lives of men and women who are indwelt by God's Spirit. Paul says that this treasure (the glory of God) is displayed in jars of clay to show that the all-surpassing power is from God and not from us. Paul follows with a litany of human pain and suffering declaring that God's fullness is seen in our helplessness.

Our text seems almost parenthetical. The litany of human suffering opens the way for the apostle to speak of his own journey and how in his experience difficulty had been translated by God's power into transforming hope.

"Therefore we do not lose heart!" (4:16). Heart language needs little explanation. We know what losing heart is. We remember moments when our plans and dreams were dashed and something at the center of our being seemed to die. Humans can endure unbelievable suffering and discouragement and somehow keep on going. But there can be moments when our inner fortress caves in. The herculean effort of yesterday is no longer possible. We have lost heart.

Paul had found some secrets.

In the Face of Death, a Source of Inner Life

"Though outwardly we are wasting away, yet inwardly we

are being renewed day by day" (4:16b).

People who met and heard Paul rarely remained neutral. They either loved him and followed him in pursuing Christ, or they hated him. Paul was a brilliant thinker who engaged people intellectually and volitionally. What set the apostle apart, however, was that he was able to speak *with* people and not *at* them. When you hear a preacher you know immediately whether he is talking with you or at you. Former generations would listen to those who talked at them. Such is no longer the case. Truth is communicated on a deeper level in which we engage people in authentic conversation.

The preacher does well to avoid the use of first person personal pronouns. Yet every preacher is communicating a great deal about his inner person. The listener can sense rather quickly whether the speaker is living in an honest relationship with himself. One of those areas of honesty has to do with mortality.

Paul was a person who had faced his own mortality. His lifestyle was dangerous by choice. He was never far from death. "For we who are alive are always being given over to death for Jesus' sake, so that his life may be revealed in our mortal body. So then, death is at work in us, but life is at work in you" (4:11–12).

This preacher did not live with a morbid preoccupation with death, but his value system and priorities took into account that everyday might be his last.

Henri Nouwen, in his book *Creative Ministry*, tells of a young priest in pastoral training. His mentor sent him to visit a patient in the hospital who knew he was soon to die. When the mentor and the priest later listened together to a tape of the visit, it was obvious that the young priest found the situation quite awkward. He was never really able to engage the patient in conversation about his impending death. The mentor suggested that it was perhaps because the priest had never come to terms with his own mortality.[1]

One of the great preachers of the past observed that he preached as a dying man to dying men. There is a compassion and realness about the individual who walks daily with a sense of mortality.

While the average TV viewer watches thousands of violent deaths in a given year, the truth is that we live in a death-denying society. It is not uncommon for children in our society to reach their teen years having never been to a funeral. I will never forget the day I walked with a young father into a little country cemetery. I stood with him while he dug a grave, placed the tiny coffin of his newborn child in it and then gently covered it. The dirt was moist with a constant stream of tears. We would live better and we would certainly be more effective ministers of Christ if we lived more honestly about death.

Is that morbid? Not at all. Paul's awareness of physical mortality was balanced with the reality of growing inner spiritual life. There was a time when his spirit had been dead in sin. Having been made to know God and love him, he was, like all the children of Adam, separated and alienated from the Creator. There was no interest in God or response to Him. He was inwardly dead. But his encounter with the living Christ brought forgiveness and a right standing with God and the invasion of God's Spirit to quicken his spirit. Not only was Paul alive to God, but his inner person was in a constant state of growth, fueled by daily impartation of divine life.

While the body was perishing, Paul was aware that the

inner person was closing in on the glory that lay ahead. This reality was a powerful element in shaping his response to the pain in his life.

Transforming Hope

"For our light and momentary troubles are achieving for us an eternal glory that far outweighs them all" (4:17).

Christians are often caricatured as pie-in-the-sky dreamers. The old saying that I heard as a boy was, that religious folk get so heavenly minded that they are of no earthly good.

When I hear such comments I wonder if those who talk that way have ever honestly considered what the Scriptures teach about God's glorious purposes for mankind. Perhaps their idea of heaven is limited to streets of gold, mansions, harps and angels. Such mental images may raise fleeting desires but will fall short of stirring life-molding ambitions.

Paul's life witness remains a sterling testimony to the power of hope to become the driving force in a person's life. Remember that this man who may well have been the greatest intellect in the history of the Western world and who perhaps has influenced our civilization more that any other, witnesses boldly and unshamedly that the great driving power in his life was a compelling desire to know the glory of God.

C.S. Lewis, the Oxford don who became a Christian apologist, made a similar confession in his little book en-titled, *The Weight of Glory*. He says there are five promises which the Scriptures hold before the believer—

1. We shall be with Christ.
2. We shall be like Him.
3. We shall have God's glory.

4. We shall be fulfilled.

5. We shall reign with Christ.

His thesis is that the rewards which the Scriptures hold out for us are the very things most deeply desired by mankind, and desires that are not filled in this life. We might expect, says Lewis, that if God is a God of order, He will create in us desires that He has designed for fulfillment: hunger/food; thirst/drink; love and affection/marriage and sex. He concludes that if we experience compelling spiritual desires—such as immortality, oneness with God, glory— and if such desires have no means to be fulfilled in this life, then we can assume that the Creator has a provision for us that we have not yet received. For Lewis, that is what heaven is about.[2]

I find his logic fascinating. And my heart resonates with it. With the passing years has come the growing awareness that life's deepest desires can never be fulfilled in this fallen world. I have been made for something that I cannot yet fully see.

Paul's conviction was not based upon mere logic or experience but rather rooted in history, in redemptive history: "With that same spirit of faith we also believe and therefore speak, because we know that the one who raised the Lord Jesus from the dead will also raise us with Jesus and present us with you in his presence" (4:13–14).

Lewis addresses the charge that it is mercenary to serve God to obtain eternal reward. Rewards can be mercenary, he argues. For instance, if a man marries a woman for money, that is mercenary because money is not the proper reward for love. But if he marries because he loves, and longs to be loved, that is not mercenary because marriage is the proper reward and end of love.

The Scriptures affirm that we were made for God's glory. Therefore to long for glory, to be driven to obtain it, is not mercenary but rather the normal pursuit of God-given desire. A.W. Tozer observed that on the whole our problem is not that we desire too much but rather are satisfied with so little. A drink or two, a little sex and a few paltry ambitions seem enough to preoccupy. God has created us to taste His glory and infinite joy. Spiritual pursuit calls for passion.

We are talking about what it was that made Paul tick. The indwelling Holy Spirit awakened desires long deadened by the rule of sin—desires that pointed to eternal glory. The hope of glory casts trouble in an entirely different light.

Notice the three things Paul says about our troubles:

1. They are light. In Romans 8:18, Paul expressed his judgment that the sufferings of this present time are not worthy to be compared with the glory which shall be revealed in us. The weight of our burdens may threaten to cave us in, but seen in the light of the glory to come they are cut down to size.

2. Troubles are momentary, says Paul. The darkness and despair that flood the soul may seem endless, but glimpsed against the backdrop of eternity, they are momentary.

3. God's grace turns troubles into tools that shape us for an eternal glory that will outweigh them all. We do not lose heart, says the apostle, because the Hope of glory transforms our troubles.

This does not mean that physical death is without spiritual trauma for the believer. In the opening verses of chapter 5 Paul uses vivid imagery to describe his ambivalence as he faced the great divide. The human body is like a tent in which we dwell. We know that it is temporary, that someday it is to be folded up and destroyed. Our faith assures us that God has a building for us, an eternal house not made with hands. He speaks of our resurrection body which will reflect His glory.

Yet Paul is honest enough to admit that while on the one hand there is within the believer a growing, identifiable longing to be clothed with God's glory, there is at the same time while we dwell in this tent, a groaning that expresses our natural fear of being unclothed from this earthly body.

It seems to me that in 5:4–5 Paul indicates that the eternal life that has already taken up residence within the believer is a foretaste of the glory to come, and that this inner life is continually growing to the point that someday it will simply swallow up this mortal flesh so that we may become what God has made us to be: "For while we are in this tent, we groan and are burdened, because we do not wish to be unclothed but to be clothed with our heavenly dwelling, so that what is mortal may be swallowed up by life. Now it is God who has made us for this very purpose and has given us the Spirit as a deposit, guaranteeing what is to come."

This is a hope that transforms. It is a settled and sure hope. The indwelling Holy Spirit is the deposit and guarantee of what is to come.

I hope you are not one of those who thinks that the hope of heaven tends to make people impractical and useless. The fact is that the vast majority of great humanitarian works have been wrought by people who were motivated by the hope of heaven.

Values Focused on the Unseen

"So we fix our eyes not on what is seen, but on what is unseen. For what is seen is temporary, but what is unseen is eternal" (4:18).

A pastor friend of mine used to say that there are just three simple things God requires of the Christian:

- to believe the incredible.
- to see the invisible.
- to do the impossible.

The incontrovertible evidence of inner spiritual life is the ability to see. The true worshiper cultivates the discipline of walking through the moments of the day with God always in view. The ability to see the invisible brings a deepening sense of reality to the pilgrim.

For the worldling the real things are those he or she can touch and hold. While he or she may allow for the presence of the spiritual, the worldling views it as less than real. On the contrary, the person of faith sees that the material world is temporary, scheduled for a fiery demise. It is the spiritual things that are eternal and lasting.

We may talk like spiritual people, but when the hard decisions come we may respond like a materialist. We believe in honesty, and hold firmly to principle, but a person does have to be practical when this much money is involved. After all what is more real, integrity or a gold Cadillac?

The educational philosophies of the last century have fed us a steady diet of the dry dust of rationalism. We have bought into the false idea that man's mind is the final judge of truth and that the material universe is the whole of reality. Things of the spirit have been filed under the superstitious, the irrelevant or at best, the speculative.

I once heard Ben Brodinsky say that the report card of the human race would look like this:

A in physics and technology
B in genetics
C or D in psychology
F in morality, ethics and the humanities

It is in the unseen things of the Spirit that our western culture has failing grades. Though secular materialism has left a younger generation without a foundation for moral and ethical belief, there is evidence of a growing spiritual hunger that could be the precursor of a sweeping revival.

People of faith are easily misunderstood. Part of the reason could be because they see what others do not see.

Dr. W.B. Hinson was immersed in fruitful pastoral ministry when he learned that he had cancer. A year later he gave this powerful testimony to his congregation.

> I remember a year ago when a man in this city said, "You have got to your death." I walked out to where I live, five miles out of this city, and I looked across at that mountain I love, and I looked at the river in which I rejoice, and I looked at the stately trees that are always God's own poetry to my soul.
>
> Then in the evening I looked up into the great sky where God was lighting his lamps, and I said: "I may not see you many more times, but, Mountain, I shall

be alive when you are gone; and River, I shall be alive when you cease running toward the sea; and, Stars, I shall be alive when you have fallen from your sockets in the great down-pulling of the universe!"

Endnotes

1. Henri Nouwen, *Creative Ministry* (Garden City, NY: Nelson Doubleday, 1971), pp. xiv–xv.
2. C.S. Lewis, *The Weight of Glory* (Grand Rapids: Eerdmans, 1949), p. 7.

CHAPTER 6

Beyond Trivial Pursuits

2 Corinthians 5:11–21

Trivial Pursuit is a parlor game that took our country by storm a few years ago. It is well suited to those individuals that have quick minds and the ability to recall details. For such people, Trivial Pursuit can be an ego trip.

I recall one of the last times I played the game. A friend was doing quite well and was more than a little impressed with his mental prowess, almost to the point of being obnoxious. Feeling some pastoral duty to help him keep his balance I said, "In the midst of your feelings of exaltation you need to remember the word *trivial.* Trivial means 'of little significance.' "

One of our first pastorates was in a small town in Kansas. Among the town characters was a farmer who spent his evenings reading a set of encyclopedias. The slightest lull in any conversation was occasion for him to dump a load of knowledge on any who would listen. I stood in front of the barber shop one day visiting with a young farmer. The walking encyclopedia joined us and sought to enthrall us

with a lengthy description of the city of Corinth, including
the harbor and other topographical details (the talk around
town was that he had never been out of the county). When
he finally walked off the young farmer commented, "That
fellow has acquired a vast amount of useless information."

It is possible to be intelligent, industrious, studious, even
erudite and still be preoccupied with the trivial. It is possible
for a church to become totally absorbed in trivial pursuits.
Our energies can be taken up with activities that only result
in making fallen people a little better. In a good many
churches what is transcendent and eternal has slipped away
and is seldom missed. All the activities and the results of
those activities can be explained by psychology or sociology.

Our text is a call to get beyond trivial pursuits. We have
noted that the Corinthians had become critical of Paul,
though he was their spiritual father. They said some rather
cutting things about the apostle. They questioned his motives, suggesting that he was in the ministry for money. They
said he lacked integrity and was not a man of his word.

Chapter 5 seems to suggest that they were also concerned
that he was a fanatic. It is not hard to see that there was some
basis for such a charge. Paul's résumé would not be attractive
to most churches today. He had been involved in a riot in
Ephesus, stoned and left for dead on another occasion, put
in jail in Philippi, run out of town in Thessalonica and
laughed to scorn by the philosophers in Athens. In Corinth
Paul was hauled into court and during a skirmish, Sosthenes, the leader of the synagogue, was injured. The sophis-
ticated people of cosmopolitan Corinth were displeased
with Paul's lifestyle. Our text could well be called the
defense of a fanatic.

Chapters 4 and 5 are somewhat of an apologia for radical

obedience to Christ. Paul's point is that Christians are citizens of two worlds. They live in Corinth, Athens, Rome, Jerusalem, and yes, in New York, Los Angeles and Centerville. They live and work and function in the culture. While they do not live by its value system, they operate within the value system.

They are citizens of heaven as well. They are kingdom people. Their eyes are fixed on a value system that is transcendent and eternal. Christians are people who see the unseen.

Believers are often caricatured as narrow people. And some of God's dear people do need to broaden their view of things. Christianity is not a narrow worldview, actually just the opposite is true. The reason that Christians are often misunderstood is that they see so much. What may seem like fanaticism may simply be the fact that believers are committed to what is beyond trivial pursuits.

Let's look at Paul's explanation of his "fanatical" behavior.

Empowered by Christ's Love

Verses 13 and 14 suggest that the apostle may have been answering the charge of fanaticism: "If we are out of our mind, it is for the sake of God; if we are in our right mind, it is for you. For Christ's love compels us . . ."

When the church of Jesus Christ is in vital, organic relationship with its Master, it is driven by a powerful centrifugal force. We experience centrifugal force in numerous ways. You may have risked one of these rides at the state fair. It is a large cylinder in which the thrill seekers stand around the perimeter. As it begins to spin faster and faster the bottom drops out. There is no danger of anyone falling because they are pinned to the inner wall of the cylinder by the centrifugal force.

John Stott, in his book on Christian mission, says that the love of God, *agape* love, is like a powerful centrifugal force motivating the church to push outward, to love, to give, to sacrifice. Why is the church always reaching out? Why missions? Why must we always go to the next village or over the next mountain? Because it is the nature of God to love and to give.

The love of Christ compels us. That is how Paul explained his behavior that seemed somewhat fanatical to the Corinthians.

On the other hand, what is most natural to fallen human nature is self-centeredness. Putting self at the center of our personal little universe creates a powerful force of gravity which absorbs us in getting, holding, grasping and preserving. When the gravity of self-centeredness holds sway in our hearts we are ultimately imprisoned by the trivial. Only the compelling love of Jesus Christ can empower the church to get beyond trivial pursuits.

My years in pastoral ministry have taken me through 38 annual missions conferences. Our denomination finances its missionary outreach through the faith promises of individual members taken at an annual missions conference in each local church. For me this conference has been a major focus in the church year, rivaled only by Christmas and Easter. In my mind this is the opportunity for the church to be confronted again with God's larger purposes in the world and renew its commitment to be part of the action. This dramatic commission calls for addressing the deeper issues of Spirit-filled living, stewardship and obedience.

With my pastoral juices approaching flood tide it was

natural for me to approach each conference with enthusiasm and anticipation. It only took two or three conferences for the painful realization to dawn that not everyone in the congregation shared my enthusiasm. As time went on I realized that numbers of people purposely planned to be away during conference week because they wanted to avoid it. As my sensitivity sharpened I realized that the missionary theme created tensions among the congregation. Though my enthusiasm has never waned, in recent years I have approached each conference with the expectation that tension would be mixed in with whatever enthusiasm and anticipation might be present.

I came to see that this tension involves the clash of two powerful forces. On the one hand the centrifugal force of God's love impelling the church to respond to the needs of lost and hopeless humanity, and on the other hand the gravitational pull of the deep-rooted self-centeredness that plagues Adam's race. There are numerous issues that uncover these conflicting forces in the life of the believer, but none so dramatic as the unfinished business of world evangelism.

For the first time since our Lord's ascension the completion of the task is in view. In the March-April 1992 issue of the *Bulletin of the U.S. Center for World Missions,* Ralph Winter presented a diagram picturing the remarkable growth of the church. In the year 100 A.D. there were 360 non-Christians on earth for every believer. That ratio has had a steady and yet dramatic decrease until there are now just 6.8 non-Christians for every believer. In that same time span the number of unreached people groups on planet Earth has diminished from 60,000 to 11,000. The completion of the Great Commission is a do-able task in this generation.[1]

Sadly, in this moment of great opportunity the church is being disarmed by an insipid universalism. Throughout our congregations are significant numbers of people who have succumbed to the pluralistic spirit of our time and who are not really sure that those who have not heard of Christ are hopelessly lost. To say that Christ is the only way to God and that people of other religions must repent and seek Christ to be saved, seems, well, radical, if not fanatical.

The Corinthians thought Paul to be a bit fanatical. His defense was that the love of Christ compelled him.

Disciplined by Stewardship

The second line of Paul's defense was that his life was disciplined by an understanding that impelled him beyond trivial pursuits: "We are convinced that one died for all, and therefore all died. And he died for all, that those who live should no longer live for themselves but for him who died for them and was raised again" (5:14–15).

The core of our faith is identification with Jesus Christ. As sinners, we know that He died in our place and, therefore, our old life is condemned and nailed to the cross. And in His resurrection power we are raised to newness of life to live no longer for ourselves but for Him. Paul describes a change at the spiritual center of our lives. There was a day when we lived for ourselves, driven by gravitational pull. Getting, grasping, holding were the high priorities, but now we have been set free by resurrection power. There is a new spiritual center where Christ is enthroned as living Lord.

Perhaps it has not occurred to you that Paul's affirmation is a stewardship statement. Since the idea of stewardship is often viewed in the narrow sense of fund-raising, I prefer to use the term management. Yet somehow I cannot bear to give up a good biblical word like stewardship. It is a concept that permeates the whole of Scripture and is used to describe the Creator/creature relationship.

God is the owner, the Bible declares. Of what? Of everything! On what basis? He created it, He sustains it by the word of His power and He has redeemed it. Everything belongs to Him.

The stewardship model designates each of us as stewards or managers. The steward manages what someone else owns. The bottom line is that God owns me and everything that I possess. Part of my rebellion as a sinner is expressed in the propensity to possess what belongs to God and allow it to possess me.

The understanding that shaped Paul's inner life and the conviction that drove him to the far reaches of the Roman Empire was that not only did God own him because He had created him, but more than that, God had bought him out of rebellion, pride and spiritual blindness through the redeeming death of His Son.

Basic to the whole idea of being a manager is that the priorities are ordered by the owner. Paul's logical conclusion was that he could no longer live for himself, but for the One who had died for him. Paul was a religious man in his younger years but he owned himself. When he haltingly stood to his feet after being smitten to his face on the Damascus road, this Pharisee was owned by God.

The parables of Jesus unmistakably and repeatedly announce that the way we manage our money in terms of God's priorities in the world is a basic issue of faith and growth. I am convinced that the fundamental factor in putting one's life together is settling the ownership issue.

Who owns what I possess? Learning to bring God the first

and the best, developing the discipline of tithing, cultivating a generous spirit, these are elementary steps in living out God's ownership in the world. It is obedience in these matters that liberates God's people so that financial considerations no longer dominate their decisions.

Pastors who do not honestly instruct and challenge God's people about managing money with God's priorities in mind may well be hirelings instead of shepherds. I have always felt it to be one of my most important obligations as a spiritual leader.

The missionary enterprise has a "fanaticism" about it. Men and women went to Africa in the early days of our mission knowing that there were more missionary graves there than missionaries. Going to Africa was not a career decision but rather a life investment choice based upon God's declared priorities in the world. They went because they were owned by another and the Owner's plans called for an invasion of the enemy's strongholds. That reasoning still persists.

They are able to go because there are servants of God who give of their resources to fund the mission. Behind the enterprise of world evangelism is a growing corps of individuals who are making radical stewardship decisions. Like Paul they understand that entering into the redeeming grace of Christ ultimately demands a conclusion which declares God as Owner. Not infrequently does one find individuals who have turned their business enterprise over to God and who run it as a servant committed to keeping God's priorities in view. To earthly minded individuals that may seem like fanaticism but it is, in fact, the logical response to redeeming love.

If there are only 11,000 people groups on planet Earth

who have yet to hear the good news, and if the task of planting the church among them is something quite manageable for the wealthy churches of the Western world, and if we leave those peoples in darkness for another generation simply because we ignore God's ownership of our lives, shall we not be liable for judgment? The parables of Jesus make it clear that unfaithful stewards must give account.

That sounds like fanaticism, you say. The Bible calls it stewardship. It was Paul's defense to his critics.

Envisioned by Spiritual Realities

Another reason that Christians can be misunderstood and perhaps thought to be a bit fanatical is because they see what others do not see. Having become spiritually alive in Christ, they are able to view the spiritual universe through the eyes of faith.

One of the realities that comes into view is the understanding that men and women have a spiritual dimension. More than that, they see that the spiritual dimension of humanity is what is real. Notice how Paul expresses this in verse 16: "So from now on we regard no one from a worldly point of view. Though we once regarded Christ in this way, we do so no longer."

What is the worldly point of view about people? Materialism posits that we are only creatures of time and space. We have been generated by natural processes, shaped by evolutionary forces, have risen higher than the other animals—but when you're dead, you're dead. Our society uses lofty language to speak of the glory of man, but the secular worldview in the end leaves mankind with no transcendent dimension, little more than an animal.

The devaluation of human life that is shattering our society is the fruit of materialistic philosophy. In a sermon Myron Augsberger once said that materialism is the narrowest of all worldviews. He called it, "this-is-all-there-is-ism."

Paul confessed that there was a time when he viewed Jesus Christ in that fashion. To Paul, the Pharisee, Jesus was only a man, a deluded and mistaken teacher, a threat to all that was precious to him. The religious zealot felt no inhibition in persecuting the followers of the Galilean. He was on his way to Damascus with orders for arrests when the risen Christ arrested him.

When his eyes were opened by new birth to view the glory of God in the face of Jesus Christ, he saw people as he had not seen them before: "Therefore, if anyone is in Christ, he is a new creation; the old has gone, the new has come!" (5:17).

In a fallen world it is easy to see people as competitors to be conquered, obstacles to be removed or objects to be used for pleasure. When our eyes are opened to view each person as a creature crafted in God's image and made to share His glory, our value system is turned topsy-turvy.

The love of Christ compels the church to address human need. Health, housing, education, poverty are needs that are addressed where believers are alive to God and motivated by *agape* love. Yet while all of these are a proper expression of God's love, none of those deal with the essential reality of human nature.

Adam's race is fallen and alienated from the Creator. The spirit has been darkened by sin and rebellion. The most urgent need of every human being is to be reconciled to God. Paul's appeal is passionate:

> All this is from God, who reconciled us to himself
> through Christ and gave us the ministry of recon-
> ciliation: that God was reconciling the world to
> himself in Christ, not counting men's sins against
> them. And he has committed to us the message of
> reconciliation. We are therefore Christ's ambas-
> sadors, as though God were making his appeal
> through us. We implore you on Christ's behalf: Be
> reconciled to God. (5:18–20)

The gospel announces that peace has been made between
earth and heaven. The alienation that cut off Adam's race
from fellowship with the Creator has been pacified. The
door for reconciliation has been opened by an incredible
sacrifice on the part of God: "God made him who had no
sin to be sin for us, so that in him we might become the
righteousness of God" (5:21).

Individuals who are convinced that the most basic human
need is to be reconciled to God, and that the means for
healing that broken relationship is found in Christ alone,
are often considered out of step by modern people whose
view of reality is earthbound.

The genteel folk in Corinth were a bit embarrassed by
Paul's extremism. They would have been happier if he had
avoided the controversy that attended his confrontational
teaching. His defense was forthright and open, compelled
by God's love, disciplined by a strong sense of stewardship
and envisioned by the spiritual realities of people destined
for eternal joy or unimaginable loss.

I heard a poignant story several years ago that says it all.
A tour group was making its way through the famed
Westminster Abbey in London. The group members, al-

ready enthralled by the soaring architecture, were fascinated by the guide's commentary describing the coronations, the royal weddings and the burial places of the famous.

There was a little old lady in the group who sported white tennis shoes and carried a large shopping bag. The guide noticed that in spite of his best efforts her mind seemed focused on other things. Finally, she interrupted the guide mid-sentence with her question, "Has anybody been saved here lately?" The guide tried to ignore her and get on with his spiel but she would not be put off. No one could miss hearing as she asked even more loudly, "Has anybody been saved here lately?"

We can chuckle at the awkward situation, but the fact is the little old lady was asking the right question. Maybe we need to ask it at our church. Clarifying the answer might help us get beyond trivial pursuits.

Endnotes

1. Ralph Winter, "Editorial," *Mission Frontiers: Bulletin of the U.S. Center for World Missions* (March-April, 1992), p. 4.

CHAPTER 7

God's Grace Is for Now

2 Corinthians 6:1–13

There are moments of spiritual insight that are so vivid and clear that they last a lifetime. One of those came to me in 1971 when I was crossing the flood-swollen Mekong River in a small boat. I had ridden all night on the train from Bangkok, Thailand, to the Laotian border. There a missionary colleague met me and my luggage and we boarded a small boat to cross the Mekong River into Laos.

The river, which flows the length of the Southeast Asian peninsula and empties into the gulf, was about to overflow its banks. Our little boat was navigated skillfully to avoid floating trees and other debris. I commented to my friend about the awesome power of the ravaging current. His brief comment was a moment of truth for me.

"Paul," he said, "if the energy in this raging river were properly harnessed it could furnish enough power to Southeast Asia to radically change the economic complexion of the subcontinent. But sadly, it flows to the gulf totally untapped."

In that moment I glimpsed a picture of the mighty grace of God flowing to the spiritual poverty of Adam's race and often wasted, totally untapped.

Listen to the urgent word Paul wrote to his Corinthian parishioners about responding to God's grace: "As God's fellow workers we urge you not to receive God's grace in vain" (2 Corinthians 6:1).

Did you notice that the exhortation is coupled with an affirming word? We are fellow workers with God. What a needed reminder! God is at work in the world. We see evidence in many places of God breaking into the affairs of human beings to work His mighty purposes. On the road to Damascus Christ had invited Paul into the arena. In the same way the apostle is reminding his colleagues in the gospel that each of them, and each of us who are believers, is called by our Lord into the arena.

Do you sense such a calling? Are you watching for our risen Lord to invade your circumstances and allow you to be a fellow worker with Him? Is there room in your life for a supernatural happening? Or is your existence totally explained by psychology and sociology?

At the moment of new birth the Spirit of God comes to take up residence in the believer. The grace of God is received. His life and power are a present resource to vitalize the inner life of His servant. Everything is there for powerful living as a fellow worker with God. But, sad to say, like the mighty Mekong River, it is possible to receive the grace of God in vain. That is, God's grace may be resident and yet flow through with little or no power being expended for His purposes. Paul's urgent word is that we must not receive God's grace in vain.

Our thesis in this study of Second Corinthians is that

Paul's openness in baring his heart before his critics allows us to see the convictions he had about ministry. Remember that we are not talking about professional ministry, but defining ministry as the joy God longs for every believer to experience in knowing that the indwelling life of God is causing his or her life to affect the lives of other people regarding their relationship to God and their eternal destiny. Each chapter of Paul's letter gives further insight as to how ministry happens.

A quick overview of the letter will immediately impress on you the frequent mention of suffering and hardship. Was Paul hoping to engender pity from the critics? Does he want them to feel sorry for him? There is no reason to suppose that. It does appear that the apostle wants us to understand that the difficult things that he experienced were not because he was disobedient or because God was punishing him. Rather, an underlying message in the epistle is that ministry takes place most often in the context of human suffering.

If difficulty and suffering were mentioned only once or only in passing, we could perhaps avoid the subject or give it little attention. But the fact is that Paul weaves it all throughout his letter beginning in chapter 1. The opening words of praise glorify the God of all comfort who comforts us in all our troubles so that we can be a comfort to any who are in trouble.

The theme of chapter 4 is that God has put His glory in clay pots like you and me. Glimpses of glory shine through as God makes us adequate in the middle of pain and difficulty. We are hard pressed but not crushed, says Paul. His argument moves to conclusion in verse 10: "We always carry around in our body the death of Jesus, so that the life of Jesus may also be revealed in our body."

There was physical suffering that Paul bore by identifying with Jesus Christ. In Paul's way of thinking it was not something to shun, nor was it hard to understand. It was a means by which the life of Christ would be manifest in His body. It is an indicator of our generation's false assumptions that there are so many books on the market trying to explain the reason for suffering.

I am not suggesting that Paul never had questions about the stressful events of his life. Nor would it be honest to convey the idea that he was so spiritual that he threw his arms open to any kind of suffering. In fact, later in the letter he describes how that three times he sought God's face about having a thorn in the flesh removed. It is natural to want to avoid pain and Paul was human, but he did understand that there is a strong tie between suffering and effective ministry.

People today who are into the "health and wealth" gospel side in with Paul's critics quite easily. Can you hear them? If God is blessing Paul's life why is there so much pain? He must lack adequate faith to appropriate the full riches God intended. We know God doesn't want His servants beaten or imprisoned. Is Paul in unbelief? Is he living below what God intends because he doesn't focus on the positive?

I can personally witness to you that one of the most difficult things about having a serious ailment is the theological problems it gives your Christian friends. Often the counsel they give is not so much designed for your comfort or up-building as much as to deal with the fact that your illness is contradicting their presuppositions about what God ought to be doing.

Paul's exhortation in chapter 6 flows from a frame of reference that has room for God's people to share the same sufferings that are in the world.

The last sentence of verse 2 is often quoted as a gospel invitation: "I tell you, now is the time of God's favor, now is the day of salvation."

The Old Testament text which Paul used as a basis for this invitation is a great Messianic text. It speaks of the coming Redeemer who will bring favor to God's people. Since it speaks of the Savior it is a fitting context for an invitation to salvation. This is the day of grace. Now is the time to believe!

Yet I am not sure that is Paul's intent. He is clearly writing to a group of believers. Verse 1 urges them not to receive God's grace in vain, a statement that would seem to indicate that they have received it already. I wonder if Paul is not using the word salvation in its broader meaning. For instance, I was saved 50 years ago as a small boy. By faith I received Christ's death on my behalf and His righteousness as my own. The gospel declares that at that moment I passed from death into life.

It is certainly biblical to speak of my salvation as a completed and settled transaction. Jesus said that the one who believes on Him has already passed from death unto life. Yet it is also true that my salvation is not finished. While I am not what I once was (praise God), it is also true that I am not yet what I shall be. The truth is that I am still being saved. By the indwelling power of Christ I am being saved from the sin and rebellion of my fallen nature and from the corruption that infects the world system. That salvation will finally be completed when with the redeemed of the ages I stand glorified in the presence of the King.

Paul's exhortation addresses three issues that are crucial to our growth:

1. The Message of Our Life Involves God's Grace Working in the Now

"I tell you, now is the time of God's favor, now is the day of salvation" (6:2b).

Someone has characterized this statement as a brief lesson in "nowology." Nowology is not a highly recognized field of study but it is a much needed discipline. Procrastination can effectively nullify the powerful work of God's grace in our lives. We can essentially receive God's grace in vain. It doesn't take disobedience or rebellion to block the effect of sanctifying power in the inner life, only putting it off or pushing it into the past.

Yes, brother, I was saved many years ago. It was wonderful. I'll never forget the joy and delight of knowing a clean heart and right spirit toward God. Oh, dear sister, my heart is looking with anticipation to the glory. Heaven will be glorious. Those are both good testimonies! Nothing to really find fault with in either of them. But, says Paul, *now* is the day of salvation. How is God's mighty power at work in your life now? That is the issue!

Are you tuned in for a bit of "nowology"? The grace of the past and the glory of the future are important chapters in our life story. But what gives the story authenticity is the *now*. Like the mighty Mekong River, is the grace of God flowing through your life without accomplishing anything of significance? Will you heed Paul's admonition that today is the day of salvation?

2. The Message That God Is Writing in Our Lives Can Be Discredited

"We put no stumbling block in anyone's path, so that our

ministry will not be discredited" (6:3).

That's graphic! When you hear the words *stumbling block,* your toe begins to ache. We have all struggled to swallow the rising anger at the individual so unthoughtful as to leave the toolbox right in the pathway to the bathroom. There is an unwritten rule that pathways should be kept uncluttered.

In the spiritual realm, the mention of stumbling blocks usually evokes thoughts of moral and ethical inconsistencies. The moral failures of numerous Christian leaders are a fresh wound in most of us. We wonder how many sincere seekers have stumbled on the pathway because of the obstacles.

I think Paul had other issues in mind; he hinted at this by listing ways we commend ourselves to other people. Many people have been helped in their witness by Joseph Aldrich's book, *Lifestyle Evangelism.* A key idea in the book is that most problems in communicating our faith are not theological, but cultural. When people are turned off by our witness, he says, it is usually not because they disagree with our beliefs. That may be true sometimes, but most often it is because they do not even understand what we believe. They are turned off by cultural messages that blind them to what the real issues are.

Some of those misconceptions might be:

- Christians are unrealistic. They do not really believe what they are talking about. It's a cop-out.
- Christians are not involved in the real world. They are off by themselves. They go to all these religious meetings and deny the real world.
- I admire the high standards that Christians have but they are not like me. Somehow they have been made

different than I am, and what they experience would not meet my needs.

- Christian answers probably work for people with no problems, but the pain and difficulty I am in requires different answers.
- Christian answers don't really work. They are just covering up; underneath they are really no different than I am.

Aldrich's thesis is that evangelism happens for the most part when our lifestyle builds bridges so that people can see us as we are. It happens best, he says, when they are not confronted first with doctrines and theological differences, but with a lifestyle that works.

It is also his contention that evangelism happens through the life of the church, not its programs, but the reality of its life in the community. It happens as Christ is incarnate in the body, as the body becomes beautiful like a bride being prepared—beautiful in its integrity, beautiful in its love for one another, beautiful in its ministry to the suffering, beautiful in its caring for the hurting. That beauty becomes the credibility for people to see its belief being worked out in action. It is important to remember that the message God is writing across our lives can be discredited.[1]

3. God's Message in Our Lives Is Commended by His Grace Being Lived Out in Our Difficulties

"Rather, as servants of God we commend ourselves in every way" (6:4).

What follows appears to be a long list of experiences in which we can commend ourselves in terms of the message God is building into our lives. As you perhaps know, the punctuation in our English translation of the Scriptures is supplied by the translator. There is no such punctuation in the Greek. Looking at this rather lengthy list we have to ask ourselves, are all the words of equal and independent meaning, or do some words qualify or modify others? I want to suggest that there are perhaps three main ideas communicated.

The first way we commend ourselves is by *endurance*. The Greek word is *hupomonee*, used 32 times in the New Testament. Often translated *patience*, it is an important concept in New Testament thought. It does not indicate a passive waiting, but rather an active response to circumstances. It has been called the divine alchemy by which pain and difficulty are transformed into spiritual maturity and character. James, the brother of our Lord, described this process in his epistle:

> Consider it pure joy, my brothers, whenever you face trials of many kinds, because you know that the testing of your faith develops perseverance [endurance]. Perseverance must finish its work so that you may be mature and complete, not lacking anything. (James 1:2–4)

Paul was able to recall numerous circumstances that had tested his endurance: troubles, hardships and distresses, beatings, imprisonments, riots, hard work, sleepless nights, hunger. Though we may not be able to identify with most of those, each of us has a catalog of experiences that give us ample opportunity to let endurance do its work. Walking into trouble with an upward look, exhibiting a quiet spirit and unmovable confidence are evidences of endurance which will turn the difficulties into spiritual grace and maturity.

Dick Phillips and his wife, Lil, are missionaries in Burkina Faso, West Africa. They were serving in the highlands of South Vietnam in 1975 when the country fell to the North Vietnamese forces; they spent several months as prisoners of war. I remember talking with Dick one night in Saigon about the possibility that any of us might become captives. He told me that he had already had such an experience as a child. Having been raised by missionary parents in China, he had been interned by the Japanese during World War II.

In that camp was a psychiatrist who later wrote a book about his experience, focusing on the responses of people in such a pressured situation. The author was not a believer at the time.

His observation was that when the people were first interned everyone responded with strong inclinations to self-preservation. From his view the Christians seemed no different than others in the beginning. Everyone looked out for number one. Selfishness was the order of the day. But, he says, as time passed the Christians began to emerge. Their deep confidence in God's sovereign purposes and the Spirit's work in their lives began to cause them to endure, to walk through the experience with dignity, a quiet spirit and generosity. He confessed that this witness challenged his presuppositions about Christianity.

Paul's list includes the matter of *Christlike conduct* in the midst of difficulty: "In purity, understanding, patience and kindness; in the Holy Spirit and in sincere love; in truthful speech and in the power of God" (2 Corinthians 6:6–7a).

When God's servant is under pressure and the thing that oozes out is Christlike response, the life message is commended to those who watch. The list here is similar to the fruit of the Spirit listed in Galatians 5:22–23: "But the fruit of the Spirit is love, joy, peace, patience, kindness, goodness, faithfulness, gentleness and self-control."

When the pressure is on, the message can be read most clearly.

Paul speaks as well of *steadfastness* in the midst of life's paradoxes. None of us escapes suffering of one kind or another. For the most part we are able to integrate it into the scheme of things so that while it is uncomfortable, it does not destroy our sense of balance. But there are events that do unsettle us, things that simply do not make sense; they fly in the face of our expectations regarding God. These are the paradoxes that defy integration into our theological framework.

> With weapons of righteousness in the right hand and in the left; through glory and dishonor, bad report and good report; genuine, yet regarded as impostors; known, yet regarded as unknown; dying, and yet we live on; beaten, and yet not killed; sorrowful, yet always rejoicing; poor, yet making many rich; having nothing, and yet possessing everything. (2 Corinthians 6:7b–10)

Like Job we glorify God most when we stare injustice in the face and declare our confidence in God's unfailing love. When genuine people are called impostors and yet continue to walk on in quiet confidence, when people beset with horrendous sorrows are able to rejoice, when those who seem to have lost everything have resources to enrich other people's lives, when folk who have little or nothing exhibit contentment and fulfillment, the grace of God is commended to the unbelieving.

I was touched by the account of a young man who sensed God's call to missionary medicine. When he completed his training he went to a North African nation where there was a dismal lack of medical care. He was offered a position on the hospital staff in the capital city where there was some semblance of the comforts of home. His vision, however, was to go to a primitive place where there was no medical help.

He hired porters to carry their supplies and he and his pregnant wife walked behind and headed into the jungle. Finally they reached a village on a little stream that seemed to him the proper place for a mission that would heal bodies and communicate God's grace. In a clearing outside the village he built a little home and a clinic where he began to treat the diseases of the villagers. They came eagerly. He invited them to a church service each Sunday but even though he clanged the bell (a tire iron on an old rim) no one came. He and his wife worshiped alone, that is until their little son was born.

The little boy was a delight to them. They watched with pride as he toddled around the clearing and explored the environment. One day the doctor noticed that his son seemed to be falling frequently. He tried to ignore it but realized that it fit the symptoms of a fatal jungle fever. He tried desperately to save his son but in short order the little boy succumbed to the tropical disease.

The doctor constructed a wooden box with his own hands and laid his son in it. He and his wife held a simple memorial service, expressed their awful grief and then he placed the box on his shoulder, took a shovel in hand and started toward the burial ground on the other side of the village.

The villagers stared as he walked through the village with the box on his shoulder. One villager followed him from a distance and watched as he dug the grave, tenderly placed the box in it and covered it with the dirt. Suddenly overwhelmed with his loss the doctor fell headlong onto the grave and began to convulse in tears.

He had no idea how long he lay in the mud but his next remembrance was a hand grabbing him by his hair and lifting up his head. There he stared into the face of a wide-eyed villager. As his head dropped abruptly back into the mud he heard footsteps running rapidly toward town and a man yelling at the top of his lungs, "The white man cries just like we cry, the white man weeps just like we weep." When the doctor banged the tire rim on Sunday morning most of the village gathered to worship with him and his wife.

God is writing a message across the life of every believer. This message has to do with the way that the mighty power of God is meeting human frailty in the suffering that characterizes the fallen creation. Paul exhorts us not to receive God's grace in vain. It is our patient endurance in difficulty and the growth of Christlike character under pressure that will commend our message to an unbelieving world.

Endnotes

1. Joseph Aldrich, *Lifestyle Evangelism* (Portland, OR: Multnomah Press, 1981), p. 40.

CHAPTER 8

Complete Your Consecration
2 Corinthians 6:14–7:1

Do not receive God's grace in vain! Such was the admonition of Paul to the Corinthian believers. The grace which every believer receives at the new birth is the Holy Spirit who comes to indwell and empower.

In the opening paragraphs of chapter 6 Paul described how this grace would manifest itself in the believer's life:

- By triumphant living in the midst of trouble and pressure.
- By character being molded in Christlikeness.
- By consistency in the tension of living in two worlds—a citizen of heaven and a pilgrim in a fallen world.

As we observed in our last study the apostle was concerned that so many of the Christians were living lives absent of any evidence of such power. The Spirit of God lived in them but this grace was being dissipated with little or no effect.

God's supply is more than adequate for effectiveness and

fruitfulness, but is often blocked by a willful heart unprepared to receive. In our text Paul points to the answer:
complete your consecration.

"Since we have these promises, dear friends, let us purify
ourselves from everything that contaminates body and
spirit, perfecting holiness out of reverence for God" (2
Corinthians 7:1).

I like the translation of the last sentence in the New
English Bible which reads, "In fear of God let us complete
our consecration." It is imperative that believers understand
that though the Holy Spirit takes up residence within us at
the moment of regeneration, and though we possess within
all the power we need to live in victory and grace, that power
will be manifest in fullness only as we allow God to possess
us wholly.

There was a retired school teacher in one of our congregations who was an able Bible teacher and exegete. Whenever
I exhorted the saints about seeking the fullness of the Holy
Spirit, she would greet me afterwards with a word of encouragement and then this comment: "Yes, Pastor, it is true
that when we are born again the Holy Spirit is *resident,* but
he must become *president.*" I like that—it rhymes nicely and
is good theology as well.

One of the works of the Holy Spirit is to make the things
of Christ real to us and to form Christ within us. That is why
Christians speak of being indwelt and filled with the Holy
Spirit and then turn around and say that Christ lives in them.
There is no confusion nor contradiction. A.B. Simpson spoke
of Christ as our holiness, our Sanctifier. Yet he spoke freely
of the Holy Spirit coming in His fullness to empower the
believer for holy living.

When we believe "savingly" upon Christ we are made holy

in Him. His righteousness is put to our account and is a covering for us so that when God looks at us he sees Jesus. We are made holy (sanctified) by the Holy One (Jesus Christ) coming to indwell us. The fact is, however, that though we may stand holy before God by Christ's righteousness, we may find that the lifelong habits of sin and selfishness continue to keep us in defeat. There is an ongoing need for God's power to be manifest in the day-to-day living out of our lives. Being made holy is not only a standing that we have before God through Christ, but an ongoing work through which our lives are empowered to live free from the shackles of sinful habits and attitudes and to revel in the freedom of being able to obey God from the heart.

Can anything be more obvious to the Spirit-enlightened heart than our total inability to make ourselves holy? We can do *nothing* to establish a right standing before God or provide the power for daily holy living—it is all from God. It is the life of the Holy One living within that is the source of our sanctification.

Yet is it evident from this text that there is a part that we play in the ongoing process of being made holy. "Let us purify ourselves," Paul says, "perfecting holiness out of reverence for God." Complete your consecration! Hear the exhortation. It is a word of hope to believers who are muddling through endless days of defeat wondering if the Christian faith really works.

What does that mean? Simpson spoke of entering into the fullness of God's provision in Christ as a crisis. The term crisis is troublesome to some people. It suggests to them the necessity of some kind of traumatic experience in order to enter into spiritual fullness.

Actually a crisis is simply *a moment that demands decision.*

The work of God's Spirit in our hearts leads us to circumstances that confront us with the choice of complete surrender to God. The crisis involves a momentous decision to surrender and is followed by an ongoing pattern of choices as we complete our consecration.

The Promises of God Call Us to Consecration

"Since we have these promises"—clearly the rationale for purifying ourselves is God's promises. Paul precedes this statement with quotes from the Old Testament to affirm God's loving intentions:

> As God has said: "I will live with them and walk among them, and I will be their God, and they will be my people."

> "Therefore come out from them
> and be separate,
>   says the Lord.
> Touch no unclean thing,
>   and I will receive you."
> "I will be a Father to you,
>   and you will be my sons and daughters,
>   says the Lord Almighty." (6:16b–18)

These promises are taken from Leviticus, Isaiah and Hosea, reminding us that all through the history of Israel there was a recurring theme: God calling the nation to respond to His love and be abandoned to Him. The idea of consecration is as great and high and wide and long as the love of God. At its center is the one great commandment: "Love the LORD your God with all your heart and with all your soul and with all your strength" (Deuteronomy 6:5).

God was saying to Israel, "I have given you all of Myself and I long for a fitting response. I want you to be holy, that is, to be of a single heart in your devotion to Me." Every ceremony and ritual, every symbol in the temple, every part of their worship was designed to convey the message that God wanted them to be wholly set apart to Him.

Every vessel used in the worship rituals in the temple had been duly consecrated. Instructions had been given for its proper cleansing, then it was set apart from all other usages such as eating, drinking, etc. And finally it was set apart and dedicated to the singular purpose of worship, filled with oil, water or wine.

At its completion the temple itself had been consecrated. The animals had been slain and the blood shed for the cleansing of the building, the priests and the nation. It was set apart from other uses. Nothing was allowed to desecrate it, not a Gentile or idol worshiper. It was dedicated and set apart to the glory and worship of God. And when the consecration was complete, God came down in a cloud and His glory filled the temple. Consecration means literally to fill the hand.

Why was the temple consecrated? Because of the promise. Jehovah had declared His intent to come and dwell among them and to be their God and they to be His people. Paul reminded the Corinthians (6:16) that we are the temple of the living God. The reason that we should complete our consecration is that the Lord intends to live in us and among us.

Consecration is first of all an act of faith. It is believing the promise of God.

Cleansing Prepares Us for Consecration

"Let us purify ourselves from everything that contaminates body and spirit" (7:1b).

We, of course, cannot purify ourselves. We have nothing inherent in our fallen human nature to deal with the moral catastrophe that has devastated us. We cannot pay our moral debt or change our character. It is God through Christ's death who has made provision for that.

But there is a part that belongs to us in the miracle of redemption. Consecration involves confession, or agreeing with God about sin—letting Him name it, accepting His judgment upon it and allowing Him to remove and cleanse it. The Apostle John exhorted first century believers to this inner integrity regarding sin:

> If we claim to have fellowship with [God] yet walk in the darkness, we lie and do not live by the truth. But if we walk in the light, as he is in the light, we have fellowship with one another, and the blood of Jesus, his Son, purifies us from all sin.
>
> If we claim to be without sin, we deceive ourselves and the truth is not in us. If we confess our sins, he is faithful and just and will forgive us our sins and purify us from all unrighteousness. (1 John 1:6–9)

Notice John's declaration that it is God who forgives our sins and purifies us from all unrighteousness. Could there be better news or a more generous offer? John makes the point, though, that God's redeeming purposes are carried out in concert with our response.

At the core of our response is integrity, honesty with

ourselves and with God about our sin. John calls it "walking in the light"—refusing to hide our failures and rebellion, and instead being open with God about our need. Confession, coming clean before God, insisting on full accounting with my own conscience—these are the responses that bring God's full measure of grace to bear upon my sin. Sins that are hidden, covered by excuses or explained away by endless rationalizing, put us in bondage and keep us from completing our consecration.

In Romans, Paul describes our integrity about sin as a death and resurrection process:

> In the same way, count yourselves dead to sin but alive to God in Christ Jesus. Therefore do not let sin reign in your mortal body so that you obey its evil desires. Do not offer the parts of your body to sin, as instruments of wickedness, but rather offer yourselves to God, as those who have been brought from death to life; and offer the parts of your body to him as instruments of righteousness. (6:11–13)

Holy living is rooted in understanding and appropriating Christ's victory. Paul says, "Count yourselves dead unto sin but alive to God in Christ." In Christ we are not victims of our fallen nature, but victors. On the basis of Christ's victory, knowing that we now are legally and organically joined to Christ, we declare our freedom and do not let sin reign in our mortal body.

Notice the emphasis in both Romans and this Corinthian passage that holiness involves both the spirit and the body. The ancient Greek philosophies sought to glorify and ennoble the human spirit but saw no connection to the behavior lived in the body. Thus their worship included "sacred" prostitution and licentiousness.

In contrast, Paul called for a response of integrity that would bring the power of God to cleanse the human heart and in the same way bring purity to the life lived out in our bodies. The cleansing or purifying of which Paul speaks calls for us to cut ourselves off from evil influences:

> Do not be yoked together with unbelievers. For what do righteousness and wickedness have in common? Or what fellowship can light have with darkness? What harmony is there between Christ and Belial? What does a believer have in common with an unbeliever? What agreement is there between the temple of God and idols? For we are the temple of the living God. (2 Corinthians 6:14–16)

Holy living involves separation. Before I can be fully joined to Christ and be wholly His, I must be cut off from whatever is incongruous with His character and holiness. This important truth has suffered from extremes on both ends. There are those who look upon holiness as simply a spiritual state that has no bearing upon one's lifestyle. We do not have to look far to see professing believers whose lives have no distinctiveness. They live in the same bondage to fleshly habits as the worldling and their value system is earthbound. They are caught up in affections that fly in the face of total commitment to God.

There are also people who see separation as a call to monasticism. For them, holy people no longer live in the world. They build walls that isolate them from any influence that might sully their pursuit of holiness. While they live on planet Earth, they endeavor to not live in the world. The worldling sees that they are different, but they are a mystery, not a witness. They do not live in the world.

In the prayer of our Lord for His disciples, He said, "My prayer is not that you take them out of the world but that you protect them from the evil one. They are not of the world even as I am not of it" (John 17:15–16).

The witness of the believer is that he is in the world but not of it. Alan Redpath used to speak of penetration without contamination. The power of holy living in the midst of a corrupt world.

Clearly, however, there are relationships and associations that compromise one's wholehearted commitment to Christ. These, says Paul, must be cut off. Don't be yoked to unbelievers. The yoke was an instrument to bind two animals together so they would walk the same path. We need to associate with nonbelievers but we must not be yoked. A yoke is an intimate relationship that necessitates the adopting of like values and goals.

I never cease to be amazed at Christians who come to me and ask me to perform a wedding for them with a person who is not a believer—someone who may worship idols or even evil spirits. They rationalize away any difficulty. Either they don't know much about God, or much about the intimacy of marriage, or they do not understand human nature.

In Corinth, idolatry was an integral part of the social system. Wedding ceremonies, family celebrations, festivals and community events were all laced with idolatrous practices. It was no easy task to remain in the world and yet not partake of idolatry. Paul's reasoning is that while we live among worldlings we must understand that there are things present in their value system that are incongruous with life in Christ. In his rhetorical questions he speaks of wickedness, darkness and idol worship.

The witness of the church is that we live in the world but we are cut off from its value system. We walk in light, we put away the practices of darkness and we serve the living God.

Cleansing prepares us to complete our consecration. Paul pointed the Corinthians to the Old Testament announcements of God's intention to live among His people and be their God. This was the reason they should complete their consecration, and cutting themselves off from sin was the preparation. Are you floundering in your spiritual walk because you endeavor to serve both God and idols? Are you involved in relationships that call for continual compromise of your commitment to Christ? There is a way out.

Consecration Is Completed by Giving Ourselves Wholly to God

I fear that for many people the idea of holiness carries negative connotations. Perhaps they have come up against those who were endeavoring to be holy by conforming their behavior patterns to legalistic rules. It is a little like trying to deal with the problem of being overweight by wearing a tight corset. It is difficult for the corset wearer to communicate any experience of freedom or joy. Self-made saints are often inflexible, critical and joyless individuals.

The fact is that holiness properly understood is the most attractive idea possible. Holiness is related to wholeness. Think about an intimate relationship to God. He declares His intent to be our Father and we His sons and daughters. Think about never being alone again.

Think about the conflicting passions that have torn your inner life every which way for so long being integrated into one life-uniting passion. Think of the power to do what you know you ought and finally being free to choose what is good.

Think of being free from the lifelong struggle to please others and being able to rest in the pleasure of our heavenly Father. Think of the joy of having a thousand petty loyalties united in one holy passion for God.

Since we have these promises, says Paul, complete your consecration out of reverence for God. Have you ever reverenced God by giving Him everything? Have you presented yourself totally to God in response to His love? "My heart is Yours to be filled with Your love, my body is Your temple to indwell and my mind is Yours to think Your thoughts." Are you afraid? Afraid that you can't keep your commitment? Make the commitment and trust God for the power to fulfill it.

Is God asking too much? I recall reading a beautiful story told by Bob Benson that helps me keep consecration in perspective. The story was published in a little book entitled, *Come Share the Being*. It goes something like this:

Remember the old-fashioned Sunday school picnics? That was back in the days before television. The pastor would announce on Sunday that everyone would meet at the park on Saturday. Everyone should bring their own food, but the Sunday school would provide free ice cream and lemonade.

You end up having to work until noon on Saturday and when you look into the refrigerator for some food to take to the picnic all you find is some stale bread and a hunk of bologna. So you slap the bologna between two slices of stale bread, dig a little mustard out of the bottom of a jar (getting it all over your knuckles), stuff the sandwich in a brown bag and head for the park.

By the time you get there the games are finishing up—the gunny-sack race, the three-legged race and other ancient evangelical traditions. The pastor stands on a table to call the people together, says grace and tells people to find a table and prepare to eat. You get your brown bag and try to find as inconspicuous a place as possible to eat your bologna sandwich. As you get settled at a table and prepare to open the brown bag, along comes a family who asks to share your table. They are carrying a picnic basket about the size of a steamer trunk.

They begin to unload and spread on a table an array of food: fried chicken, potato salad, tossed salad, baked beans, apple pie and chocolate cake. About that time the lady looks over and notices your bologna sandwich. "I have a great idea," she says. "Why don't we just put all our food together and share?"

Can you imagine yourself saying, "Oh no, I couldn't give up my whole bologna sandwich. I love bologna sandwiches. And besides it's all I have." It doesn't seem fitting to talk about sacrifice when God invites us to come share His being.[1]

Is there some reason you cannot complete your consecration?

Endnotes

1. Bob Benson, *Come Share the Being* (Nashville: Impact Books, 1974), p. unknown.

CHAPTER 9

The Good Fruit of Repentance

2 Corinthians 7

Paul's Corinthian letters are a vivid reminder (as if we need one) of the tensions that can characterize local church life and the resulting need for firm and effective leadership. Churches are made up of people in varying stages of maturity; disagreements, opposition and criticism are inevitable—and are often directed at the leadership. These tensions will test the mettle of any leader. The ability to walk through the fire with grace adds height to a leader's stature.

The first Corinthian letter illustrates the kinds of challenges that face church leaders. Paul confronted the issue of a member having an illicit affair with his father's wife. He pressed for discipline, then firmly and lovingly called for correction of both theological irregularities and behavioral shortcomings.

His leadership drew mixed reviews. There was a storm of criticism against Paul and ugly accusations about his fitness to be an apostle. Church discipline is often like that—which may explain why it is so frequently avoided! In an earlier chapter I mentioned Larry Crabb's observation that one of the most destructive factors to community in church life is our penchant for self-preservation. When leaders choose self-preservation and avoid the pain of church discipline they allow the sense of community to be undermined and reap more pain in the long run.

Paul was faithful and took the risk. His second letter to the Corinthian believers allows us to witness a leader's gracious response. The apostle sought to engender understanding by allowing them to see into his heart. His openness and vulnerability have enabled us to uncover some of the principles of ministry. Our text today is the portrait of a leader who refused to allow the fires of criticism and opposition to alter his loving concern for the welfare of God's people.

The personal and conversational tone of the seventh chapter of Second Corinthians lends itself to teaching a good many lessons that each of us could learn about personal relationships. I am touched by how freely Paul expresses affection and joy for them in spite of the pain he was enduring from their criticism.

> Make room for us in your hearts. (2 Corinthians 7:2)
> We would live or die with you. (7:3)
> I have great confidence in you. (7:4)
> I take great pride in you. (7:4)
> I am greatly encouraged; in all our troubles our joy knows no bounds. (7:4)

It is obvious that Paul was not a "process" person. His focus was not on short-term relationships but long-term results. The mature spiritual leader's first concern is not for the immediate happiness of the sheep but for their growth and safety. Such love has the power to cover a multitude of sins.

Knowing that his letter of discipline and correction could well engender negative reaction, Paul had sent Titus to visit them and to bring back a report. Titus reported that while the majority of the believers were exhibiting a repentant attitude there remained a recalcitrant minority who were vocal in their criticism of Paul. Though the report was not totally positive Paul did not miss the opportunity to use Titus' visit as further reason for joy and affirmation.

In verses 5–7 he speaks of the comfort that he received from Titus' return and his report on those in Corinth who felt concern for him. In the last paragraph the apostle brags on his spiritual children:

> In addition to our own encouragement, we were especially delighted to see how happy Titus was, because his spirit has been refreshed by all of you. I had boasted to him about you, and you have not embarrassed me. But just as everything we said to you was true, so our boasting about you to Titus has proved to be true as well. And his affection for you is all the greater when he remembers that you were all obedient, receiving him with fear and trembling. I am glad I can have complete confidence in you. (7:13–16)

The result that brought joy to Paul's heart was the response of repentance. His comments on their repentance are a pointed reminder to 20th century Western Christians for whom godly sorrow is a foreign idea. Dr. John Hunter of England says that one of the reasons the church finds itself powerless today is a missing word in our message: repentance.

The Scriptures are replete with commandments to repent. Yet our gospel formulations and invitations to believe are strangely devoid of any mention of it. Jesus told a story about a runaway son who squandered his inheritance in riotous living. When famine came and he found himself feeding pigs and eating their leftovers, he realized that the servants in his father's household were treated with generosity and care. He decided to go home and plead with his father to receive him as a servant.

Jesus said that he arose and came to his father. Here is the picture of repentance. The Greek word *metanoia* speaks of a radical change of heart which turns a person around and heads him back to the Father. In our Lord's story the father received his wayward son and led the household in joyous celebration. It was the father's unconditional love that opened the door to restoration but it was the son's change of heart that led him home.

Dr. Hunter says that most people today see faith as a mere intellectual activity. There is no repentance, no change of heart. They make mental assent to certain truths about Christ but they remain in the pigpen.

Our Need of Repentance

The letter is addressed to believers. Are you wondering why Christians should need to repent? If a person repents when they come to Christ in faith, why should repentance be needed again? The answer is simple. All of us are like sheep. We sing it in one of my favorite hymns.

Prone to wander, Lord I feel it,
Prone to leave the God I love.

We are like sheep—we tend to wander from the truth. When believers find themselves far from God it is usually not because they have intellectually decided to no longer believe or follow God. Rather the case most often is that we wander from the truth. We wander in our heart's affection. We may still hold orthodox views but the attitudes of our hearts have wandered far.

I have a friend whose pastoral ministry and personal life have been marked by a good deal of pain. Patterns which persisted for a long time had resulted in a trail of broken relationships including his marriage. In recent years God has been bringing a remarkable healing in his life and in a recent letter he gave this reflection: he said that up to this point in his life it never occurred to him that pastors need to repent. A common but costly misunderstanding.

The believers in Corinth had wandered from the truth. While there were some doctrinal irregularities involving ideas regarding Christ's return and the proper use of spiritual gifts, the major issues were matters of the heart. They had wandered from the truth that the church is the body of Christ in the world and ministers by Christ's love being manifest in caring relationships. Instead, the church was divided into competing parties. Body life was characterized by strife, bickering, power grabbing and backbiting. It was ugly.

Symptomatic of their spiritual waywardness was their refusal to deal with crass immorality among them. One of their members was sexually involved with his father's wife. Division is ugly and debilitating; immorality un-confronted and allowed to spread leads to spiritual death.

The Corinthians had wandered far from the truth. They needed to repent. I hope repentance is vital to your understanding of the Christian life.

The Cause of Repentance

What brought about the change of heart among the Corinthians? They were awakened by the pain inflicted by Paul's letter. Note that the letter was painful for Paul as well:

> Even if I caused you sorrow by my letter, I do not regret it. Though I did regret it—I see that my letter hurt you, but only for a little while—yet now I am happy, not because you were made sorry, but because your sorrow led you to repentance. (7:8–9a)

Paul felt regret when his letter caused them pain. The regret was momentary, however, because the pain brought godly sorrow.

> For you became sorrowful as God intended and so were not harmed in any way by us. Godly sorrow brings repentance that leads to salvation and leaves no regret, but worldly sorrow brings death. (7:9b–10)

Are you aware that, as we stray spiritually, God's way of awakening us is often to wound us in spirit? It is a wound that God uses to produce godly sorrow, which will lead to a change of heart.

Solomon said, "Wounds from a friend can be trusted" (Proverbs 27:6a). Job declared, "Blessed is the man whom

God corrects; so do not despise the discipline of the Almighty. For he wounds, but he also binds up; he injures, but his hands also heal" (Job 5:17–18).

In his tenderness God brings conviction. His Word brings a sense of sin, godly sorrow and contrition. About 600 years ago there lived in Norwich, England, a lovely lady who had little light but a great heart. She wrote only one brief book but it has left a mighty impact. Her name was Lady Julian. She prayed once, "O God, please give me three wounds: the wound of contrition, and the wound of compassion, and the wound of longing after God." Then she added, "This I ask without condition."

The text says that there are two ways to respond to hurt. It can lead to worldly sorrow. Worldly sorrow expresses itself in resentment, rebellion and even bitterness. The end of worldly sorrow is spiritual death, hardness of heart.

It is easy to wander from the truth and let our hearts become cold and indifferent. We may remain correct and proper in our doctrine but lose a sense of passion for God or love for our brethren. The hurts in our lives beget anger and grudges. The unconfessed wrongs become a roadblock to fellowship and any sense of ministry drys up. We continue to go through the motions but nothing is really happening.

In his compassion for us God sends a wound. His design is to awaken us and prick our conscience. There grows within us a longing for things to be right. But it is hard to change, it is difficult to humble ourselves, our pride screams against confession.

It is a critical moment. Godly sorrow will lead to repentance. In Revelation, the One who stood among the lamp stands made this charge against the church at Ephesus, "You have forsaken your first love." And the remedy prescribed? "Remember the height from which you have fallen! Repent and do the things you did at first" (Revelation 2:4–5).

It is godly sorrow that leads to a change of heart.

The Fruit of Repentance

"See what this godly sorrow has produced in you: what earnestness, what eagerness to clear yourselves, what indignation, what alarm, what longing, what concern, what readiness to see justice done" (2 Corinthians 7:11a).

Does Paul's description stir something deep in your soul? It would be hard to find a better picture of revival. When revival comes, when the Spirit of God breathes upon the church, the first evidence is the repentance of believers. The roadblocks are down and confession and forgiveness flow freely. People's hearts are awakened to fresh longings for God.

We were pastoring the International Protestant Church in Saigon in 1972 when a much-prayed-for revival broke out at the Nhatrang Bible School. As the students fanned out into the village churches on the weekends, fires of revival were lit across the countryside. Among just one of the tribes 60 churches were affected, with some 6,000 Christians being greatly stirred and evidencing a change of heart.

The reports that came spoke of new joy, warmth and devotion toward God, a note of praise and gratitude. There were new attitudes toward other believers expressed in concern, forgiveness and generosity.

Near the village of Dalat on the side of a mountain there was a shortage of tillable land. A significant piece of land had lain fallow for years because two of the village elders, both of them Christians, had a grudge between them. When the Spirit of God moved among the church these men were broken and confessed their sin. They had a radical change of heart and were united to one another. In a miracle of grace, the fallow land was once again free to bear fruit.

The breakthrough between these two men brought a fear of God and sensitivity to sin among all the villagers. Fetishes, idols and hidden things of the old life were brought to be burned. Such is the fruit of repentance.

Is it possible that once again repentance could become a normal part of church life and Christian understanding in our culture? Could we be awakened to our coldness of heart and be wounded in spirit so that godly sorrow may produce its good fruit? What would it take to make us willing to pray like Lady Julian?

CHAPTER 10

The Style of Ministry

2 Corinthians 8–9

When I was a kid my dad used to take us to the barbershop. It is not one of the happier memories of my life. The long wait while three boys had their ears lowered seemed interminable. The barber's hand clippers were sometimes a bit dull and pulled the hairs rather than cut them. There were reasons why our barber only charged 25 cents when the going rate was 50. When I got old enough to realize how my hair looked, the choice of barbershops became a rather hot issue in our family. Three little boys were discovering style.

Have you noticed that barbers are out and "hair stylists" are in? We are a style-conscious generation. I had little idea when I was 10 years old that my passion for a 50-cent haircut represented one of the cultural issues of our time. Marshall McLuhan dropped a bombshell a couple decades ago with his dictum, "the medium is the message." His insight raised our awareness that the style in which something is done or said becomes part of the message.[1] This insight has given birth to the science of public relations and imaging and as a result style has evolved into an obsession.

Wearing clothes has now become the fine art of making a statement. Automobiles have ceased to be a mere mode of transportation. One's vehicle is seen as an important statement of status or even sexuality (I am not quite sure just what the message of my rusty Pontiac is). You can't live in our time and ignore style. Part of being a thoughtful Christian and a faithful steward is learning to relate to our culture and yet not become a slave to style. We must not forget that modesty and simplicity are valid style statements as well. I am afraid that the content of the gospel message is often confused these days by the way it is packaged.

The Apostle Paul was not unaware that style affects the impact of the message. He was, in fact, concerned that the first century believers cultivate a specific style for their ministry. Remember that in our study of Second Corinthians we are viewing ministry as the work of God's Spirit in which the indwelling life of Christ in the believer touches the lives of others, affecting their relationship to God and their eternal destiny.

The way that we relate to people shapes the message of the gospel as it is played out in our lives. There is a style that befits the ministry, a way of relating that enhances the message. That style, says Paul, is generosity.

It is possible for our style of people relationships to be in total contradiction to the message God is writing across our lives. If our style is stingy and begrudging, then the message lacks power and authenticity. Generosity is the style that complements the ministry.

Chapters 8 and 9 of Second Corinthians are Paul's plea for believers to cultivate a lifestyle of generosity. The circumstances that occasioned this exhortation were down-to-earth and practical but it is evident that the apostle wanted to use the situation to cultivate attitudes that he saw as basic to spiritual effectiveness. The circumstances had to do with the believers in Jerusalem. Severe persecution was taking place against the Christians and one of the effects of the opposition was that the believers were often denied the means of making a living.

To show their oneness with the saints there, Paul was encouraging each of the churches he had planted to take up an offering to help alleviate the suffering in Jerusalem. Though some among the Jewish believers were critical and suspicious of Paul, he wanted the Gentile churches to feel part of the larger body of Christ. It was not his intention to plant independent congregations.

Apparently the people in Corinth had been quick to promise to give such an offering, but had not gotten around to it. It is a bit surprising to me that Paul, having been accused of being "in it for the money," was bold enough to press for an offering for the saints in Jerusalem.

In my mind this indicates two things about the apostle. One is that he had a quiet, settled confidence in his own integrity and motives. He would not allow criticism to derail his commitment to their spiritual growth. It also testifies to the strength of Paul's conviction that generosity is essential to spiritual development. He was not going to allow anything to deter him from addressing the truth that would help them grow.

So on the surface these two chapters are an appeal for an offering to help suffering saints. Behind it, however, is the rationale for a lifestyle of generosity that Paul saw as essential to the authenticity of the gospel message. Let's remember that giving money is only one small way to express generosity. The style that complements ministry calls for giving time, surrendering privacy, making room in our lives for needy people, opening our home, making our gifts and abilities available and taking a servant role. With that in mind let your heart hear Paul's appeal to generosity as a lifestyle.

The Model

I am interested that Paul chose both a divine model and a human model. This is the way that spiritual growth takes place. Christ is the ideal but our motivation to follow Him is enhanced by seeing truth fleshed out in another human being. God's generosity shines fully in the person of His Son: "For you know the grace of our Lord Jesus Christ, that though he was rich, yet for your sakes he became poor, so that you through his poverty might become rich" (2 Corinthians 8:9).

The Advent season brings a yearly reminder of the condescension of our Lord. He was rich. We have only a faint idea of His wealth. He was the glory of heaven, the delight of the angels, the center of the unceasing worship of all creation. All the fullness of wisdom and knowledge rested in Him. As the infinite, immutable, self-sufficient Creator He had no needs. He was complete, fully at rest. He was rich.

He became poor. How poor? He was born in a cattle stall, wrapped in rags and laid in a manger. He laid aside His omnipotence to become a helpless babe. He surrendered eternity to be bound by time. He grew up in an insignificant town working as a carpenter. He owned no home, had no where to lay His head, and had only the clothes on His back. He died as a criminal and was buried in a borrowed tomb. He became poor.

He did this, says Paul, that we might be rich. How rich? By His grace we are offered forgiveness and freedom from sin's bondage, new birth and the hope of eternal life. We are indwelt by God's Spirit and as children of God are partakers of His fullness. We are joint heirs of Christ's inheritance and set apart to share His eternal glory. By His poverty we have been made rich.

Every grace and virtue finds its source in the divine nature. Discuss anything of lasting consequence and ultimately it will lead to reflection upon the nature of God. Why generosity? Because it is the nature of God to be generous. We know of His goodness because *He became poor*. Paul's call to a generous lifestyle began with a divine model.

But there was also a human model. The human model finds its source in the divine fullness. The human model translates the eternal into our time zone. Paul pointed the Corinthian believers to the churches of Macedonia. Notice that in 8:1 Paul affirms that the generous spirit of the Macedonians was a gift of God's grace. It is not the nature of Adam's race to be generous. Sin turns us in on ourselves and makes us slaves to our own desires. It is God's grace that sets us free to be givers. Paul goes on to describe God's grace in the Macedonians:

> Out of the most severe trial, their overflowing joy and their extreme poverty welled up in rich generosity. For I testify that they gave as much as they were able, and even beyond their ability. Entirely on their own, they urgently pleaded with us for the privilege of sharing in this service to the saints. And they did not do as we expected, but they gave themselves first to the Lord and then to us in

keeping with God's will. (8:2–5)

Do you see the principle of ministry working its power through the Macedonian churches? The poverty of these believers became the base for a powerful witness of God's grace. Whole congregations can become models and mentors to other congregations by their obedience to God.

So Paul boldly sent Titus to Corinth to urge them to complete their commitment to take a benevolent offering for the suffering saints in Jerusalem. Paul was careful and kind in his approach but he was dogged in urging them to give.

> But just as you excel in everything—in faith, in speech, in knowledge, in complete earnestness and in your love for us—see that you also excel in this grace of giving.
> I am not commanding you, but I want to test the sincerity of your love by comparing it with the earnestness of others. (8:7–8)

Generosity is contagious. When others give to us we are challenged to break out of our self-centered posture and trust God. When we pastored the International Protestant Church in Saigon during the war years I was invited to speak at one of the tribal churches of the Bamboo Cross people who lived in the highlands near the city of Dalat. These people had suffered at the hands of the Viet Cong and had been forced to flee their village 19 times and start over.

As we approached the hastily built village we noted that it was surrounded by two barbed wire fences with poisoned bamboo stakes sticking out of the ground between the fences.

Their humble homes were constructed of old boards scavenged from packing crates. At the center of the village was the simple church building adorned with a bamboo cross.

It was an unforgettable experience to worship with this people of vibrant faith and courageous spirit. The greatest impact, however, was their boundless generosity. After the stirring service the tribal believers asked us (a party of about a dozen) to stay for dinner. With grace and simplicity they served us a delicious chicken stew. Knowing how much a chicken cost in Vietnam and how little money they had, their generosity was overwhelming and remains a fragrance that keeps challenging my heart.

The Maxim

The last part of chapter 8 is Paul's instruction about the logistics of taking the offering. Note his concern that it should be handled in a way so as to be above criticism or suspicion. He was sending Titus to oversee that process and with him another faithful servant who would accompany Titus in delivering the funds to the proper destination. Paul's rationale was that he was taking pains to do what is right not only in the eyes of the Lord but also in the eyes of men (8:21).

Jesus told parables about managers who mishandled the master's money. The newspapers carry similar stories almost daily. Paul's carefulness is a good reminder to us that no matter how confident we feel about our own motives before God, or how sure we are of the integrity of our colleagues, good stewardship requires procedures to guarantee that things are done right in the eyes of men as well.

In the opening paragraph of chapter 9 Paul's keen understanding of human nature comes through. He spoke of how he boasted to the Macedonian churches about the Corinthian believers' eagerness to help and their readiness to give an offering. It was for this reason, he said, that he sent Titus and his colleague to oversee the taking of the offering so that the Corinthians would not be embarrassed should the Macedonians find that they had not followed through on their intention. Yet he made it clear that his goal was a generous gift, not a grudging one. It was in this context that the apostle stated a principle that is built into the nature of things. His point was that generosity is related to the law of sowing and reaping.

> Remember this: Whoever sows sparingly will also reap sparingly, and whoever sows generously will also reap generously. Each man should give what he has decided in his heart to give, not reluctantly or under compulsion, for God loves a cheerful giver. (9:6–7)

Just like the law of gravity or the laws of thermodynamics there are moral principles built into the fabric of the created order. These moral maxims operate just as unerringly as what we call natural law. There is a law of sowing and reaping. What you sow determines what you reap. To sow sparingly is to reap sparingly, to sow with generosity is to reap generously. There is a style that befits Christian ministry. Generosity puts us in the flow of God's gracious outpouring upon His people and allows His grace to multiply our fruitfulness.

Jane Raffloer served as a missionary in Zaire for most of her adult life. Her fun-loving, vibrant, generous spirit won the hearts of her African colleagues. Her availability and quickness to give of herself unleashed a flow of God's grace in her relationships. In 1986 Jane came down suddenly with a strange fever and before they could get her to adequate medical help she died. It seemed to all who knew her a tragic loss.

Her family was not in sympathy with her commitment to Africa. When they heard of her death their predictable response was, "A terrible waste of a very talented young woman." Several months later her partner in ministry returned from Zaire and stopped by to greet Jane's family. They were overwhelmed when she showed them pictures of Jane's funeral. Over 3,000 people were present to honor her memory. Her brother commented, "There are not many people in the world that have 3,000 people at their funeral." Having a huge crowd at one's funeral is not the ultimate success, but such a response for an individual whose lifestyle was humble service, says something about sowing and reaping—and generosity.

One of my least favorite TV programs (a fairly long list) is "Lifestyles of the Rich and Famous." The celebrities of our time are often known for how much they have been able to amass. In the long run, the people whose lives have lasting impact are those who are noted for how much they have been able to give. You can ignore God's laws but you cannot escape them. What you sow is what you reap.

The Motivation

The last part of chapter 9 is an appeal based upon the faithfulness of God. As we have observed, the character of God is both the model and the motivation for godliness. A glimpse of God's character is the impetus for a generous spirit. How can I afford to give? Who will care for my needs if I focus on the needs of others? Verse 8 is one of the great statements of Scripture to encourage believers to trust: "And God is able to make all grace abound to you, so that in all things at all times, having all that you need, you will abound in every good work."

Reflect for a moment on Paul's portrait of God's grace. God is able. How can we picture the limitless resources of God? Sketch in your mind's eye an infinite, boundless ocean of grace. All the giving God does leaves His resources unaffected. No matter what the need God is able.

But, says Paul, God is able to make all grace abound toward you. Now visualize the infinite ocean of grace overflowing in a stream that pours itself into your small vessel. Your vessel is small and finite, it cannot begin to hold the stream of God's grace that flows from the boundless ocean of His fullness.

The immediate result of God's out-poured grace is that in all things and at all times you will have all that you need. A striking thing about this text is the frequent use of the word *all. Webster's Dictionary* uses a third of a column dancing around the idea of "all" but none of it approaches the clarity of the little fellow who was asked what all means, "All means all and that's all it means."

We are continually beguiled by the sirens of technology and management that insist that, given time and money, all human needs can be met. We are somehow blinded to the fact that every new technology brings with it pain and distress and in the end most human needs are unmet. The truth is that we were made for God and the deepest needs of the human heart are met only in Him. All is a superlative word but not an exaggeration. In all things and at all times, having all that you need—such is the fullness of God's grace.

There is also an ongoing result of God's grace being poured into our vessel. Paul says, you will abound in every good work. Now the picture is complete. The infinite ocean of God's grace is overflowing in a stream that fills your small vessel, and it is filled to overflowing so that it showers everything around it with good works.

Here is a graphic portrayal of generosity. Notice that our finite human vessel has both an intake and an outflow. God's grace flows in so that in all things we have all that we need, but then it flows out to every good work. Are you with me? Now suppose you put a lid on the outflow of your vessel. Once the outflow is blocked the vessel can receive no more from the stream of God's grace. Clearly our ability to receive from God's bounty hinges on our availability to be a channel of blessing. God is able! But is He able to make His grace abound in us when there is no way open for it to overflow to others?

Jesus said that if we give it will be given to us—"pressed down, shaken together and running over" (Luke 6:38). The wise man observed in the Proverbs that there are those who give and yet prosper, and those who hold too much and it tends to poverty (11:24). You can see why Paul was so dogged in taking steps to lead his followers into a lifestyle of generosity.

Notice what it is that God promises and what He does not promise. God does not promise that everyone is going to be rich. It is clearly not God's purpose for everyone to have lots of money. There is a good deal of preaching these days that sells this false doctrine. Often the come-on is that if you send money to our program, God will make you rich. It doesn't say that in the Scriptures.

It is not God's will for everyone to have lots of money,

but it is God's will for every believer to be generous. What does God promise? He promises that if we will be generous He will see that we always have plenty to give.

> Now he who supplies seed to the sower and bread for food will also supply and increase your store of seed and will enlarge the harvest of your righteousness. You will be made rich in every way so that you can be generous on every occasion, and through us your generosity will result in thanksgiving to God. (2 Corinthians 9:10–11)

Wait a minute, you say. The text does say that God will make you rich in every way. But remember the context is not about getting but about giving. The true riches which God wants to give us are the intimate knowledge of his character and the joy of having God's fullness ministered to others through us. God does say that if we seek to be generous He will guarantee us enough to always be able to give.

If we are willing to be generous with our time, God will give us more time so that we can make room in our lives for needy people. If we are willing to be generous with our privacy, God will somehow make it possible for us have enough of it to keep giving. And, of course, the same is true of money.

God's generous nature is a powerful motivating factor that impels us to share His character. There is another motivating truth that Paul addresses. He says that our ministry, that is, our communication of the grace of God, will be greatly enhanced by generosity:

> This service that you perform is not only supply-
> ing the needs of God's people but is also overflowing
> in many expressions of thanks to God. Because of
> the service by which you have proved yourselves,
> men will praise God for the obedience that accom-
> panies your confession of the gospel of Christ, and
> for your generosity in sharing with them and with
> everyone else. And in their prayers for you their
> hearts will go out to you, because of the surpassing
> grace God has given you. Thanks be to God for his
> indescribable gift! (9:12–15)

Why should believers be generous? First, says Paul, it will
be the means of supplying the needs of God's people. But the
overflow of it will be the expressions of thanks to God.
Further, says the apostle, your service to others will authenti-
cate your confession and men will praise God for your
obedience. The overflow of God's grace in your life will cause
others to overflow in expressions of praise and thanks to God.

One of the methods that has been greatly used in financ-
ing the missionary enterprise has been "faith promise"
giving. Dr. A.B. Simpson is looked upon as the father of
this concept, which he used in the great missionary conven-
tions that he organized in the late 19th century to stir the
church in its response to the Great Commission. It was this
passage of Scripture that led Simpson to the idea of encouraging people to plan ahead in their missionary giving
and pledge what they did not yet have in hand.

In his *Christ in the Bible Commentary* he emphasized the
fact that Paul encouraged the Corinthians to plan ahead so
they would be prepared to be generous in their offering for
the saints in Jerusalem. The text mentions that they had

planned a whole year for this offering.

Simpson's rationale for missionary pledge giving was rooted in this text:

> This surely is the very method which God has led us to adopt in these great offerings; namely, to lay upon the hearts and consciences of God's children the claims of Christ, the needs of the world and the obligations of giving liberally to send the Gospel everywhere, and also encourage them to form the largest purposes and plans of giving and even sacrificing in the spirit of a generous love and a lofty faith, and then deliberately to go to work by labor, prayer and sacrifice to gather the means thus pledged day by day until the purpose shall have become an actual performance.[2]

In the early days of The Christian and Missionary Alliance, the appeal to the missionary task was made to people of many denominations. Dr. Simpson was not asking them for their tithe, which he believed should be given to their local church. He was asking for sacrificial giving, for monies to be committed that they did not yet have in hand. The basis for such a bold commitment was the faithfulness of God. One hundred years of effectiveness testify to the validity of this principle. Not only has it financed the bold initiatives of the modern missionary movement but it has brought spiritual growth to those who have practiced it.

But there is even more, as Paul declared in this text. People's hearts will go out to you in prayer because of the surpassing grace God has given you. God wants each of us to be a minister. The core of that ministry is that God comforts us in all our troubles so that we can be a comfort to any who are in trouble. You can know the joy of being a significant influence in the lives of other people—an influence that will make an eternal difference. There is a style that gives validity to our ministry. Generosity is the style.

I am reminded of a delightful encounter which I had with Dr. Robert Smith who taught philosophy at Bethel College for many years. I had stopped by his house, hoping to schedule him to minister at our church. He graciously invited me to visit for a few moments. I was struck by the simple lifestyle that was evidenced in their home. They were missionary people to the core and shaped their value system around their commitment.

Our conversation touched on the subject of giving and he offered to tell me of a recent adventure he had experienced. I was eager to hear.

It seems that after many years with the same overcoat his wife had finally convinced him to buy a new one. When he got it home and hung it in the closet beside his old one he realized how badly his old one looked. Shortly after this a new student came by the house to see him. It was a bitter cold Minnesota day and the student had no coat. He chided him for being out on such a day without one, then realized the student had just come from California and likely did not own one.

In a moment of generosity he offered to give the student one of his and walked toward the closet with the intent of offering his old coat. As he made his way there God began to talk to him. He felt like God was saying, *Why don't you give him the new coat? That is what I would do. If you give him the old one don't do it in My name!* With some reluctance, he confessed, he took out the new coat and presented it to the grateful student. He said that he found a surge of joy in doing so but some disappointment that it had been so hard.

A couple days later he went downtown to speak at a Christian businessmen's luncheon. He wore his old coat, of course. The host helped him take off his coat and hung it up for him. When the luncheon was over the host asked if he had a few moments to spare. He took Bob down the street to a men's clothing store and asked if he might purchase an overcoat for him. Bob did not refuse the offer and went to a rack to look at coats about like the one he had recently purchased. "No," said his host, "let me choose one for you." Bob showed me the cashmere wool overcoat that was far more costly than he ever imagined owning.

It seems to me that the secret of the powerful ministry which Bob and his wife had was an authenticity that radiated from their lifestyle of generosity.

The apostle's exhortation ends with a paean of praise: "Thanks be to God for his indescribable gift!" (9:15). What is the gift? Why it is Christ, of course! Yes, it is in Christ that God has given us everything. In sending His Son, the Creator gave us the greatest of all gifts. But don't fail to see the context. Because of this indescribable gift of God's Son we are able to know the richness of being giving people.

Endnotes

1. Marshall McLuhan, *Understanding Media: The Extensions of Man* (New York:McGraw-Hill, 1964), p.7.
2. Albert B. Simpson, *"Christ in the Bible"* Series Vol. XVIII (Harrisburg, PA: Christian Publications, Inc., n.d.), p. 111.

CHAPTER 11

Secrets of Ministry

2 Corinthians 10

The mention of the word *secret* immediately piques one's curiosity. Perhaps it appeals to our longing to be on the inside of things. As children mature and move toward a greater degree of independence, the keeping of secrets is one of the ways they express it. They are, of course, frustrated and horrified at times by younger siblings who still want to tell everything they know. Families with young children have very few secrets—usually a lot fewer than they think! Family and personal secrets are usually information that we do not want anyone, or only a select few, to know.

There is another way that we use the word *secret* that relates closely to the biblical idea of *mystery*. The Scriptures use the word *mystery* to describe truths that God has built into the nature of things. A mystery, or secret, is something that is hidden. For the most part it is not something that is not to be known, but rather something that is known only through spiritual understanding or will be known only at the proper time in God's redemptive plan.

Paul wrote to the Ephesian believers about such a mystery:

> In reading this, then, you will be able to under-
> stand my insight into the mystery of Christ, which
> was not made known to men in other generations
> as it has now been revealed by the Spirit to God's
> holy apostles and prophets. This mystery is that
> through the gospel the Gentiles are heirs together
> with Israel, members together of one body, and
> sharers together in the promise in Christ Jesus.
> (Ephesians 3:4–6)

The kingdom of God is a mystery. It is not that God does
not intend it to be known; rather, it is a spiritual reality that
can only be grasped by the Spirit-illumined mind (John
3:3). Often the mysteries of God have to do with things that
are by nature contrary to fallen human nature.

For me, playing golf is that kind of a mystery. I grew up
playing baseball and the natural inclination I have is to swing
the club like a baseball bat and try to hit the ball as hard as
I can. There is a *secret*, a *mystery*, to golf that I have not
discovered. It is not a secret in the sense that it cannot be
known, but it is a secret in that it is contrary to my natural
instincts. If I am ever to learn the game of "pasture pool," I
will have to surrender my addiction to baseball instincts and
adopt a different mindset.

It is in this sense that I use the term "secrets of ministry."
There are some things about God affecting other people's
lives through us that are secrets. It is not that God does not
want us to know these things, but rather they are contrary
to human nature and therefore can only be known through
spiritual understanding. Chapters 10, 11 and 12 of Second

Corinthians deal with these secrets. I am not suggesting that Paul set out to write a treatise on the secrets of ministry. Rather, I am suggesting that as the apostle bared his heart to the believers in Corinth in an open and vulnerable fashion, he was illustrating truths about ministry that are paradoxical to us.

The "secret" that is illustrated in chapter 10, I believe, is submission. In chapter 10 Paul addresses the matter of his coming to Corinth for another visit. He had written a letter of discipline and correction. As we have observed, it was not well received. The people had responded by criticizing Paul and questioning his qualifications as an apostle. When he sent Titus to mediate the situation, the majority of the people had repented, but there was a recalcitrant minority who remained belligerent.

Now as Paul considered revisiting Corinth he was anxious for the believers there to understand his view of spiritual ministry. Chapters 10 and 11 will be difficult to grasp if we do not make allowance for figures of speech. Taking the Scriptures literally (that is, they mean what they say) does not disallow figures of speech. The Holy Spirit breathed divine revelation through human instruments but the vehicle was language. And figures of speech are one of the ways that language conveys plain truth. If after our son does a sub-par job of washing the car, I say with tongue in cheek and my voice dripping with sarcasm, "Great job, son," I am speaking just as literally and plainly as if I complained of a lousy car wash. So look for satire and tongue in cheek as Paul challenges the attitudes of the Corinthian believers:

> By the meekness and gentleness of Christ, I appeal
> to you—I, Paul, who am "timid" when face to face

with you, but "bold" when away! I beg you that
when I come I may not have to be as bold as I expect
to be toward some people who think that we live by
the standards of this world. For though we live in
the world we do not wage war as the world does.
(10:1–3)

Apparently the attitude of the recalcitrant minority in
Corinth was, "Let Paul come; he is bold in his writing but
he is nothing to fear in person!" Paul alluded to this attitude
in verse one and then uncovered the false assumption
behind it. The carnal Corinthians supposed that spiritual
leadership was rooted in personal power.

Paul affirmed that it was just the opposite. Though we
live in the world we do not wage war as the world does, he
asserted. How does the world wage war? In the world when
you are attacked, you counterattack. When people oppose
you, you undercut them. You use intimidation, sarcasm,
manipulation or any other fleshly weapon to get your way.

It was this kind of warfare that the Corinthians were
expecting from Paul. Their impression was that though his
letters were weighty, in person he in fact was a lightweight
and they would easily nullify his power plays. It is always
a sad day when God's people square off with one another
to wage war with the weapons of this world. When they
do, the devil is the only winner. There are times when you
can almost hear him in the corner of the sanctuary laugh-
ing with glee while the saints slay each other with fleshly
weapons.

Paul was saying to those who opposed him, "If you think
I am coming with worldly weapons of personal intimidation, you are wrong. Our weapons are not the carnal

weapons of this world."

> The weapons we fight with are not the weapons
> of the world. On the contrary, they have divine
> power to demolish strongholds. We demolish argu-
> ments and every pretension that sets itself up against
> the knowledge of God, and we take captive every
> thought to make it obedient to Christ. (10:4–5)

Paul understood the dimensions of spiritual conflict, how
it is that God wants to affect our lives. He wants to change
our attitudes, to demolish the strongholds that we put up
against Him. He has in mind to knock down our arguments
and confront us with the knowledge of God so that our
thoughts are captured by Christ.

What is the weapon in the hand of His servants that causes
such victories to be won? I believe that the weapon is
submission. "No," you say, "the weapon is prayer." It is true
that we often quote these verses as a rationale for prayer. It
is certainly true that the spiritual warfare in the heavenlies
is won on our knees. In Ephesians 6:18, after Paul outfits
the believer with the whole armor of God, he exhorts prayer
and supplication for all the saints. Prayer puts us on the
battlefield where the conflict of the ages is in full array. It is
my contention, that while prayer is the means by which we
wage war, our secret weapon is submission. Prayer, I believe,
empowers us to wield God's mighty weapon.

It seems to me that when there is conflict among believers
the saints tend to be much in prayer. That is good—it puts
them on the battlefield with the true enemy, the evil one.
But often, I fear, those prayers are attempts to coerce God
into a power play against a fellow saint. Believing prayer

will, on the other hand, lead us to take up the powerful weapon of submission. It is by this weapon that strongholds are demolished and thoughts brought into captivity to Christ.

The reason I am calling submission a secret is because it is hidden in the sense that it is so contrary to human nature. To believe that submission is a spiritual weapon by which God's glory triumphs is totally stupid to Adam's nature. We can easily think of a thousand other solutions to conflict before the thought of submission comes to mind.

I want to make what at first may seem a radical statement. The statement is this: the only way to bring positive change in a strained relationship is by submission. If you are in disagreement with another person, you can use the weapons of the world to coerce and intimidate and to get your way. It may feel and look like you have won, but nothing in the relationship has changed—except that the heart of the other person has hardened a little more.

What opens the door for God to come into a situation, and perhaps even to use your life to effect change in another, is submission.

Submission to God

Submission to God opens the door to effectual prayer. Sometimes we are much in prayer for God to change another person. It is possible, you know, for prayer to become quite a selfish exercise. Saying prayers can become an attempt to manipulate God into fulfilling our selfish aims. When we don't like someone it seems natural to bang on God's door with the request to change him or her. After all, if God wants me to be happy, then changing my neighbor will be a great step in that direction.

Submission opens the door for me to invite God to do not what I want, but what He wants, in my life and in the life of the other person with whom I may be in conflict. It is not just saying prayers that resolves conflicts. Such praying may be another form of manipulation that unknowingly walls God out of the situation. What brings resolution to interpersonal conflicts is mutual submission to God, submission that results from believing prayer—believing because it is rooted in Scripture and has God's glory as its goal.

Are you thinking that here comes another sermon on wives submitting to their husbands? I am not honing in on that particular relationship though there are few places where submission is more needed than in the intimacy of lifelong commitment between man and woman. Someone has characterized marriage as an unconditional commitment to an imperfect person. In this relationship that demands self-giving love from fallen sinners, prayers that do not lead to submission are not going to change very much.

In the almost 40 years of prayer meetings in which I have been involved as a pastor (and 20 years growing up), a major prayer focus was wives praying for their unsaved husbands. I have often wondered how many of those prayers were aimed at getting God to change their husbands and how many were petitions seeking for Spirit-empowered submission that could loose God's grace in their marriage. I obviously have no way of knowing that, but insights into a good many marriages suggest that prayer is often a substitute for submission instead of a petition to enable it.

Submission to Others in Christ's Name

I am not suggesting that submission to God is alone the duty of the wife. It is true that in the biblical analogy the husband is the Christ figure and the wife is the Church figure so that submitting to her husband as the Church submits to Christ is her special privilege, just as the husband's special privilege is to lay down his life for his wife, as Christ did for the Church. Neither the husband nor the wife can fulfill the high calling of living out the heavenly truth in their marriage relationship without profound submission to Christ. Fulfilling their roles will necessitate occasions when each submits to the other (Ephesians 5:21).

This obedient submission to Christ and the boldness to submit to another person in His name, unleashes the power of God's grace to disarm fleshly weapons and bring every thought into obedience to Christ.

At our youngest daughter's wedding our son-in-law, who was officiating, used this insightful quote: "Submission is learning when to duck so God can hit your husband." Actually that fits well in all relationships. When we are able to submit to God in a given situation, and submit to another person as Christ's servant, we open the door for God to bring direct pressure upon that individual.

Much of the frustration in our lives comes from our belief that we can change people. Write this across your mirror so you see it every morning when you study your own countenance: *You can't change people!* God *can* change people, and one of the ways He does that is when we submit and let Him change us first.

I remember an occasion in one of our first pastorates. Our Sunday dinner was interrupted by a knock at the door. It was one of the women of our congregation who was obviously agitated. Her husband was not a believer and she was angry at him because he was asking their young son to work in the family business even though it was Sunday. In the heated discussion that ensued she told him she was going to go see the pastor and get his opinion on what might be the right thing to do. So she told her story and then announced that she was ready to go home and tell her husband what I thought should be done. I felt like Solomon facing the two mothers who both claimed ownership of the same baby.

After breathing a silent prayer to God, I told her that she should tell her son that it was good to not work on Sunday and to honor the Lord by resting and worshiping, but that a higher principle was to obey his father. She thought my answer was foolish and told me so, but finally agreed that she would do it.

She later told me that when she got home she called her son in from where he was working. Her husband followed and stood with his hands on his hips as if to say, "Well, what did that crazy preacher have to say?" While the father stood there she told her son that the preacher said it was good not to work on the Lord's day but it was more important to obey your father. She said that her husband turned every color and then stomped out. Her son went back outside to work but soon returned. When she inquired as to why he was not working, he replied that his father said he didn't have to work on Sunday if he felt it was not right. The next Sunday the husband was in church sitting with his family.

Submission and Authority

It is interesting in the text that while Paul refuses to respond to the threats of the Corinthians with fleshly weapons, and appeals to Christ's authority, he does not hesitate to stand in his authority as an apostle.

> You are looking only on the surface of things. If
> anyone is confident that he belongs to Christ, he
> should consider again that we belong to Christ just
> as much as he. For even if I boast somewhat freely
> about the authority the Lord gave us for building
> you up rather than pulling you down, I will not be
> ashamed of it. (2 Corinthians 10:7–8)

Paul went on to say that though he did not mean to
frighten them with his letters, he did want them to understand that he would be the same in person as he was in his
letters. It is obvious that there is an authority that is not
incongruent with submission. People today tend to carica-
ture submission as a doormat mentality that destroys personal dignity and self-worth. Not in Paul's understanding.

He understood that he was an apostle, called by Christ to
plant the church among the Gentiles. He was not afraid to
confront people with truth and boldly call them to
obedience to Christ. Notice that Paul defended his ministry,
his calling as an apostle, but he did not defend himself. His
ministry flowed out of submission to Christ, and that
enabled him to submit to the Corinthians as Christ's servant. His submission would disarm their fleshly weapons.

In his book *Corporate Lifecycles*, Ichak Adizes gives the
following helpful definitions:

> Authority—the legal permission to make decisions.
> Power—the ability to punish or reward people by
> withholding or giving rewards or affirmation.
> Influence—the ability to motivate people to do
> what they ought without using authority or power.[1]

There is an authority that God grants to those He calls to leadership: apostles, elders, husbands, fathers and mothers. It is their responsibility and calling to see that the decisions are made that will hasten God's purposes among those whom they lead. Adam's fallen nature is easily drawn toward power. We want to use what authority we have to coerce and change people to our liking. And as we well know, power tends toward abuse and corruption.

Influence—spiritual influence—is the secret of ministry. Motivating people to do the right thing because they choose to is what brings glory to God. Such influence is gained by submitting to Christ and to those whom Christ has placed in authority over us.

It amazes me how many spiritual leaders wonder why they have so little influence with those under them and are not able to see that it relates to their lack of submission to those over them. Keeping ourselves in submission to Christ and to the authority of those over us in the Lord is a basic issue in all ministry.

One of the congregations I pastored confronted this issue. The constitution of the denomination clearly called for the district superintendent to work closely with the board in the process of seeking a new pastor. For almost two years the local church leaders ignored the superintendent while they searched for a pastor. Not surprisingly, they found the congregants less than submissive to their leadership during the process. When they finally came under the superintendent's leadership I was the first candidate sent and was promptly called. Some of the people saw a clear message in the circumstances.

Christ calls every believer to ministry. He wants to touch the lives of other people through His indwelling presence in His people. One of the secrets of effective ministry is submission. It is a secret because it runs counter to our natural inclinations and is only grasped by spiritual understanding. It is by putting away the fleshly weapons of gossip, slander, character assassination, intimidation and the like, and submitting to God that His power is loosed to demolish strongholds, arguments and every pretension that sets itself against the knowledge of God and take every thought captive to make it obedient to Christ.

Endnotes

1. Ichak Adizes, *Corporate Lifecycles: How and Why Corporations Grow and Die and What to Do about It* (Englewood Cliffs, NJ: Prentice-Hall, 1988), pp. 147–153.

CHAPTER 12

Developing a Taste for Humble Pie
2 Corinthians 11

Rejection is one of life's most painful experiences and for that reason the underlying fear of it can often bring spiritual paralysis. Rejection is what a person feels when his or her marriage partner pursues another lover, or what parents feel when children rebel and choose another value system, or what any one of us feels when the spoken or unspoken covenant of friendship or partnership is violated by disloyalty.

All of us have tasted the bitterness of rejection, probably at quite a young age. Children can be cruel to one another and be quick to violate friendships on a whim in order to please another. You can probably recall a number of such events from your childhood.

Everywhere I go I meet people who are emotionally or spiritually paralyzed. They have suffered painful rejection along the way and the fear of further rejection is so great that they have coped by withdrawing from the field of relationships. Many of these people received their wound in the context of the church. What makes it even more painful for them is that somehow they supposed that it would never happen among God's people. The church is a covenant community made up of individuals who have been joined in faith to Christ and in Him are united as a body in fellowship with one another. The depth of the covenant relationship makes rejection or disloyalty not only possible but all the more painful.

I have preached to congregations that were devastated because their pastor, whom they had learned to love during years of ministering together, had accepted a call to another church. Though they intellectually understood that he was answering the call of God as best he could discern it, they still felt the pangs of rejection.

Likewise I have sat and wept with pastors who after years of investing themselves in the life of a local church were asked to resign. Being fired from any job carries enough rejection to challenge one's inner resources to the fullest. But these pastors looked to their congregations as spiritual children. Many of the relationships were as spiritually intimate as those with their own families. Spiritual ministry is a kind of covenant relationship. Spoken or unspoken, when it is violated by what appears to be disloyalty it is freighted with grief.

It was just such a circumstance that was part of the Apostle Paul's relationship to the believers in Corinth. When Paul arrived the first time in the cosmopolitan metropolis of Corinth he did so with weakness, fear and trembling (1 Corinthians 2:3). He had experienced rather traumatic encounters in Philippi, Berea, Thessalonica and Athens. In Corinth he was rejected by the Jews and hauled into court. The church that was born there in pain was for Paul made up of his spiritual children. It was his fatherly love for them that had motivated him to take the risk of sending a letter of correction.

When the letter brought a negative response and then a barrage of criticism, Paul had to feel rejection. That was small stuff, however, compared to what came later. When Judaizing teachers came to Corinth the believers followed them and began to make unfavorable comparisons between them and Paul. Since this second letter of Paul's to the Corinthians was an epistle from the heart, we are able to witness how God's servant responded to rejection.

We have approached our study of Second Corinthians addressing the idea of ministry as the overriding theme—not pastoral ministry or missionary ministry, but God working His grace in each believer's life in a way that communicates Christ's life through them to others. Anytime you open your heart to others and invest in their lives, you risk rejection. They may not receive your ministry, or they may respond to Christ and begin to grow only to attach themselves to another person as they seek spiritual nurture. They may compare you unfavorably to the other person and may even tell you so—in Christian love, of course.

The last part of Second Corinthians 10 and all of chapter 11 is the section in which Paul responded to their rejection. It is a difficult passage for the reader to grasp. One can easily be disturbed by the frequent use of the word "boast." It seems evident that Paul was speaking to them tongue-in-cheek and made use of satire and a play on words in an effort to get behind their mental roadblocks and talk to their hearts.

In our consideration of this section of the epistle I have spoken of the secrets of ministry. We are defining *secret* as

it is used in Scripture—not something that cannot be
known, but rather something that God intends us to know
but because it flies in the face of fallen human nature, can
only be known by spiritual understanding. In the first part
of chapter 10 we observed that Paul's authority in addressing
the Corinthians' rebellious attitudes was rooted in his
profound submission to Christ. Submission is God's road
to spiritual authority. It is one of the secrets of ministry.

In this passage there is another secret addressed: humility.
This is the secret that enables us to experience rejection and
keep our balance. It allows us to invest our lives in others
and appear to lose, and yet keep perspective and keep giving.
The surface issue in the rather lengthy passage is Paul's
concern about being compared to the false teachers who
were beguiling the hearts of the Corinthians. The underlying issue, I believe, is Paul's meekness and humility, which
are demonstrated in his godly response. While we trace
Paul's line of reasoning in his appeal to the Corinthians let
us watch for insights about his heart attitude and the
powerful secret of humility.

In the present climate of image making, inflated egos,
self-assertiveness and the idolizing of celebrities, humility
tends to get short shrift. It is not seen by most people to be
a virtue, I'm afraid. Self-denigration, lack of confidence or
inability to accept affirmation is often mistaken for
humility. A definition that I believe fits the biblical model
is "a realistic view of oneself from God's perspective." It is
realizing on the one hand that I am only one of billions of
people whom God loves and cares for, but on the other hand
I am loved by the infinite Creator.

Meekness, I believe, is the way that humility is fleshed out
in human relationships. It has nothing to do with weakness.

Rather, meekness is a resourceful inner strength that enables one to respond with gentleness and steadfastness in the midst of opposition, criticism or rejection. It grows out of being able to see oneself as God sees me.

Paul's Humility Grew Out of His Settledness in God's Calling

Seeing people that he loved in Christ being seduced by false teachers and then having himself unfavorably compared to them had to be more than painful for Paul. The feelings of helplessness and powerlessness would tend to evoke anger and perhaps provoke a bitter attack. Notice Paul's measured response back in chapter 10.

> We do not dare to classify or compare ourselves with some who commend themselves. When they measure themselves by themselves and compare themselves with themselves, they are not wise. We, however, will not boast beyond proper limits, but will confine our boasting to the field God has assigned to us, a field that reaches even to you. We are not going too far in our boasting, as would be the case if we had not come to you, for we did get as far as you with the gospel of Christ. Neither do we go beyond our limits by boasting of work done by others. Our hope is that, as your faith continues to grow, our area of activity among you will greatly expand, so that we can preach the gospel in the regions beyond you. (10:12–16)

If Paul's measuring stick had been self-imposed, being compared unfavorably to other teachers would likely have

put him in despair. But Paul's measuring stick was the call
of God upon his life. Therefore the baseline question was,
am I fulfilling what God called me to do? He was not
measuring himself by his own standards. Most of us have
expectations of ourselves that are unconsciously being
programmed by the conflicting demands of a thousand
other people. When we measure ourselves subjectively by
the inner measuring stick we are easily victimized by unfair
criticism.

Paul had been called by Christ to be an apostle to the
Gentiles. He was deeply aware that God had chosen him
before he was born and that all his religious attempts at
righteousness had utterly failed (Galatians 1:15). He was an
apostle by the grace of God even though he was, as he saw
it, the chief of sinners.

So for Paul the question was not, am I as good as the other
teachers or am I as good as I think I ought to be, but am I
fulfilling the task of being an apostle to the Gentiles? Thus
he felt free to "boast" to the Corinthians that he had come
that far and that the church had been planted among them.
You can sense Paul's wholesome realism. He saw himself as
a faithful servant but he was aware that the Holy Spirit was
the Lord of the harvest. The congregation in Corinth was
not his church but Christ's body. Though he felt a pastoral
responsibility for them he knew well that it was Christ who
had built the church in Corinth and it was Christ who
would keep it. Humility is wonderfully liberating.

The consumer mentality that drives our economy finds
its way into the church. The expectations of congregations
are skyrocketing out of sight. People want the best in
teaching, child-care, music, preaching, etc. and they let you
know if they don't get it here they will go where they can

get it. And they do go, after giving you a rundown of unfavorable comparisons with . . . well, you fill in the blank. I talk rather frequently with pastors who are smarting from the pain of having their preaching compared to Chuck Swindoll, their leadership ability to Robert Schuller, etc. I think I can recall a few antacid nights if I try a bit—or maybe even if I don't try. I don't know who Chuck Swindoll gets compared to, but be assured that he has antacid nights just as you do. The only escape for any of us who are God's servants is a realistic view of ourselves in terms of God's calling and our faithfulness to that calling.

Another secret to Paul's remarkable balance was the dimension of his calling. The Corinthians were beloved to Paul but they did not fill his vision. He could see beyond them. In fact, his concern for them was not that they were part of his personal kingdom but rather that God intended for them to be a launching pad for taking the gospel to the regions beyond. People of limited vision are tempted to be possessive. They fight little wars and are consumed by petty jealousies. On the other hand it is amazing how a global vision can nullify the sting of petty criticism. Paul had a big vision. That vision enabled him to be a big man in the midst of small criticism. That's another powerful reason for missionary passion.

Paul's advice to us is, " 'Let him who boasts boast in the Lord.' For it is not the one who commends himself who is approved, but the one whom the Lord commends." (2 Corinthians 10:17–18). Humility grows out of settledness in God's calling.

Humility Is Expressed in Godly Jealousy

On the surface the idea of godly jealousy appears to be an

oxymoron. We tend to think of jealousy as a cousin of the green monster envy. Webster says jealousy is apprehension of the loss of another's exclusive affection. It is usually thought of as the expression of selfishness and insecurity. When that is the motivation, jealousy is destructive.

We are a bit mystified when God declares His jealousy for His people. God is concerned for the exclusive affection of His people. Does God have an ego problem? Is He insecure? Is that why He is jealous? God is perfect. He doesn't need any of us. He is not the richer for having our love or the poorer for not having it. He is jealous of our love because He loves us and longs for the best for us. And He knows that loving Him with all our hearts is what will bring the greatest joy and blessing. God's jealousy for our affection is motivated by His longing for our good. Godly jealousy, then, is not an oxymoron but a concern for the affection of another that is motivated by God's loving intention for His own.

Paul's careful and balanced response to the painful rejection by the Corinthian believers is related to godly jealousy:

> I hope you will put up with a little of my foolishness; but you are already doing that. I am jealous for you with a godly jealousy. I promised you to one husband, to Christ, so that I might present you as a pure virgin to him. But I am afraid that just as Eve was deceived by the serpent's cunning, your minds may somehow be led astray from your sincere and pure devotion to Christ. (11:1–3)

Paul's understanding of the human element in gospel communication was clear. He wrote to the Thessalonians,

"You became imitators of us and of the Lord" (1 Thessalonians 1:6). He knew well the deep and joyous affections that are part of discipling people in Christ. There is nothing quite so rewarding as knowing that God is using your life to affect others in their spiritual journey. It is easy to feel possessive about such a rewarding experience. When people follow us because they are drawn to Christ in us, we must be sure that we help them transfer that trust and affection to Christ. Like John the Baptist we see that He must increase and we must decrease (John 3:30, KJV).

It is clear that for Paul the issue was not the loss of the Corinthians' affection for him, but rather the loss of their devotion to Christ. He used the example of Eve being deceived by the serpent to picture the cunning ways in which their new teachers were leading them astray from devotion to Christ. Because these teachers were preaching another gospel Paul saw that the believers' rejection of him would in fact be a step toward rejecting Christ:

> For if someone comes to you and preaches a Jesus other than the Jesus we preached, or if you receive a different spirit from the one you received, or a different gospel from the one you accepted, you put up with it easily enough. But I do not think I am in the least inferior to those "super-apostles." I may not be a trained speaker, but I do have knowledge. We have made this perfectly clear to you in every way. (2 Corinthians 11:4–6)

The Judaizers used the name of Jesus but they were pointing the believers not to faith in the redeeming work of Christ but faith in the keeping of the law *and* in Jesus Christ.

Paul did not look upon that as a mere difference in theological emphasis; it was the preaching of another Jesus. The law keepers are still with us but there are many other Jesuses being preached today. When religious rituals, church membership, cultural behaviors or speaking in tongues become an added prerequisite for saving grace, another Jesus is being preached.

While those who preach the deeper life affirm the gifts of the Holy Spirit being exercised as *He* wills, they have been dogged in their commitment that the gifts of the Spirit (or any other emphasis) shall not eclipse the revelation of God's fullness in Christ. It had to hurt when the Corinthians unfavorably compared Paul to the false teachers, but his concern was a godly jealousy for their devotion to Jesus.

Notice in verse 6 that Paul acknowledged that he was not the gifted speaker that the new teachers were, but that he possessed a knowledge of God that had been the means of their coming to faith. Paul's jealousy about them was not regarding their affection for him, but for their devotion to Christ. A realistic view of oneself before God opens the door for godly jealousy that empowers a bold appeal for people to be devoted to Christ.

Paul had come to Corinth as a tentmaker; that is, he chose to support himself financially by pursuing his trade (that is where we get the term "tentmaker" for a self-supporting missionary). Paul had taught the churches that they should support their teachers. A servant is worthy of his hire, he asserted. But he chose not to accept such help for himself so that no one could accuse him of ulterior motives. Apparently the false teachers who had come in after him sought to use this against him. Their argument was that Paul was not a true apostle because he was not supported by the church. That is why in this letter (11:7–12) Paul was bold to "boast" about his love for them which he had expressed in not wanting to be a burden.

It is painful when people in whom we have invested our lives spiritually begin to move away from us. Humility enables us to be motivated by a godly jealousy that keeps the focus on devotion to Christ.

Humility Is Not Impressed with Credentials

The false teachers who had come to Corinth apparently were impressive individuals. They flaunted their credentials and were quick to point out their superiority to Paul. People do tend to be like sheep. The Corinthians were easily herded into the new fold of the Judaizing teachers. Paul had simply been "out-gifted" and "out-credentialed" by the competition.

Our first reaction to that idea is complete surprise. How can anyone outshine Paul? He is our hero, our model, our measuring stick for missionary valor and dynamic leadership. What's wrong with these people in Corinth? Are they blind?

We need to consider that Paul's résumé would likely not do well with most search committees for churches or Christian ministries. His record includes riots, being stoned and left for dead, imprisonment, court cases, controversy. There are a few groups, perhaps, who might be looking for a radical disciple as a leader but most are looking for stability—and ability. In such a context Paul may not rate well these days and apparently his stock in Corinth was slipping badly.

Paul's realistic view of himself with God allowed him to speak forthrightly and boldly about his "credentials." It seems to me that he was not trying to show that his credentials were superior to those of the false teachers, but

that in God's order of things credentials are of no consequence. God has a measuring stick that makes ours irrelevant. This last section of chapter 11 is somewhat
tongue-in-cheek:

> I repeat: Let no one take me for a fool. But if you
> do, then receive me just as you would a fool, so that
> I may do a little boasting. In this self-confident
> boasting I am not talking as the Lord would, but as
> a fool. Since many are boasting in the way the world
> does, I too will boast. You gladly put up with fools
> since you are so wise! In fact, you even put up with
> anyone who enslaves you or exploits you or takes
> advantage of you or pushes himself forward or slaps
> you in the face. To my shame I admit that we were
> too weak for that! (11:16–21)

Don't miss the note of satire in Paul's words. He admitted
that in his boasting he was not talking as the Lord would,
but as a fool. He had apparently been called a fool by the
false teachers and the critics who followed them. His calling
himself a fool was a play on words and a means of pointing
out the foolishness of their being enslaved and misused by
the slick operators who professed to be apostles.

It was then that Paul bared his heart perhaps more fully
than any other time and allowed them to view his real
credentials. It seems to me that he was not trying to show
that his credentials were superior to the new teachers in
Corinth, but that in the strange ways of God's kingdom the
foolish things are transformed to His glory. Listen carefully
to the credentials of a man who planted the church across
eastern Europe:

What anyone else dares to boast about—I am speaking as a fool—I also dare to boast about. Are they Hebrews? So am I. Are they Israelites? So am I. Are they Abraham's descendants? So am I. Are they servants of Christ? (I am out of my mind to talk like this.) I am more. I have worked much harder, been in prison more frequently, been flogged more severely, and been exposed to death again and again. Five times I received from the Jews the forty lashes minus one. Three times I was beaten with rods, once I was stoned, three times I was shipwrecked, I spent a night and a day in the open sea, I have been constantly on the move. I have been in danger from rivers, in danger from bandits, in danger from my own countrymen, in danger from Gentiles; in danger in the city, in danger in the country, in danger at sea; and in danger from false brothers. I have labored and toiled and have often gone without sleep; I have known hunger and thirst and have often gone without food; I have been cold and naked. Besides everything else, I face daily the pressure of my concern for all the churches. Who is weak, and I do not feel weak? Who is led into sin, and I do not inwardly burn? (11:21–29)

Was Paul boasting? Does this passage uncover a chink in his armor? Was his wounded pride breaking through? I think the answer is no.

Paul had once been a proud man. He spent his early years pursuing a righteousness that was his own based upon the keeping of the law (Philippians 3:9), until he was apprehended by Christ on the Damascus road and faced with the life-changing truth that he had been chosen from birth and saved by grace. He understood at the moment that he was chosen for apostolic ministry and that his calling had nothing to do with his life of law-keeping and good works but that he had been chosen at birth out of the grace and foreknowledge of God.

Paul, who had persecuted the church out of hatred for Christ and who saw himself as the chief of sinners, felt privileged to suffer for Christ. It seems to me that the litany of Paul's suffering was not a statement of his credentials to compare himself with others, but rather a genuine confession of the gospel of grace in which God chooses us on the basis of grace and exhibits His glory through our weakness. Notice Paul's comment that concludes the litany of his suffering: "If I must boast, I will boast of the things that show my weakness" (11:30).

This summary comment brings us to the third secret of ministry: God ministers His grace through our weaknesses (chapter 12). Paul had nothing to feel proud about. He had surrendered his credentials on the Damascus road. It was this realistic view of himself as God saw him that enabled him to keep his balance though suffering rejection by those whom he had loved in Christ. Humility is one of the secrets of ministry. It is a liberating gift. It empowers God's servants to suffer rejection and still keep giving.

CHAPTER 13

Strength and Weakness

2 Corinthians 12

Masochist! That is the term used to describe a person who finds some perverted pleasure in inflicting pain upon himself. The normal human response is to avoid pain if at all possible. One of the things that seems radical about the New Testament writers is that they speak of pain and suffering as a normal part of living, and what's more, at times as friends to be welcomed. Such ideas fly in the face of the value system of our society.

Francis Schaeffer observed that the number one value of the American culture is personal peace and comfort.[1] It is really more than a desire: most of us view it as a right. We are quick to vote out of office any government that cannot provide it or to sue the professionals that do not deliver it. And of course, it follows that if God loves us, and if He is powerful, He will take steps to insure our comfort and peace. This assumption not only sets the stage for disappointment with God but also blinds us to the powerful role that pain plays in our spiritual growth.

We have noted in our study of Second Corinthians that

pain is a major subject woven all through the epistle. In this
very personal letter Paul has bared his heart to the believers
and in doing so has allowed us to view his understanding of
God's work in our lives. In chapter 1 we saw that the most
basic idea of ministry is that the God of all comfort comforts
us in all our troubles so that we may be a comfort to any
who are in trouble.

In chapter 6 the idea is reinforced with the affirmation
that God's grace is most evident in our lives through our
patient endurance in the midst of difficulty. One can't miss
the point that it is not our strengths that are the raw material
for effective ministry, but rather our weaknesses. What Paul
has stated from a number of perspectives, he now illustrates
from his own spiritual journey.

> To keep me from becoming conceited because of
> these surpassingly great revelations, there was given
> me a thorn in my flesh, a messenger of Satan, to
> torment me. Three times I pleaded with the Lord
> to take it away from me. But he said to me, "My
> grace is sufficient for you, for my power is made
> perfect in weakness." Therefore I will boast all the
> more gladly about my weaknesses, so that Christ's
> power may rest on me. (12:7–9)

It is not difficult to identify with the experience Paul
described. We have all had occasions when we have faced
difficulty, a loss, an illness, circumstances that have hindered
or confined us. We responded by saying to God, "Lord,
something needs to be done about this, and the thing that
needs to be done is to remove it." What could be more
obvious? God is powerful and able to do it. He is good and

would want to do it. To remove it would solve all my problems.

So we prayed and believed, but it didn't happen. We were not delivered, the circumstances were not removed. We may have found like many others, that when our circumstances seemed to contradict what we understand about God, one of our greatest trials came from our Christian friends.

Like Job's comforters they come and assure you that if you just had more faith, if you would just confess your secret sin, if . . . then this thing would be removed. What makes such speculation dangerous is that there is some truth in it. Sin *can* hinder our prayers, unbelief *can* rob us of God's blessing. But most often behind this advice lie presuppositions that are unbiblical and downright cruel.

It is easy to quote promises that God made to the nation of Israel in the old covenant and draw the conclusion that God's blessing is always expressed in terms of health and material prosperity. Old Testament Israel tended to see God's blessings on them in terms of national fulfillment and material wealth.

Scripture is clear that God's purpose in this age is to call forth a spiritual body of believers, a pure and spotless Bride prepared to share the glory of the Son. God's first concern with us is purity of heart. When the lawyer asked Jesus what was the greatest commandment, He answered, "Love the Lord your God with all your heart and with all your soul and with all your mind and with all your strength" (Mark 12:30). There are principles which when understood and obeyed can unleash God's power in us for His glory.

We have spoken of these principles as spiritual *secrets*— not that they are unknowable, but that they fly in the face of our natural inclinations and can only be known through spiritual understanding. The third such secret we observe in Paul's letter is the redeeming nature of suffering.

God Is Willing to Use Suffering for Our Maturity

I have said all this because I want us to see that as much as God loves us, He is willing for us to suffer in order to bring us to spiritual maturity and to keep our hearts where they ought to be. A.W. Tozer used to say that God wants us to be happy but He wants us to be holy first so that we can be happier longer.

With that in mind, let's look at the apostle's experience. God called Paul to a large and demanding task: the planting of the church among the Gentile nations. It was not only a consuming task but a painful one; persecution, deprivation, imprisonment, abuse and defamation were constant companions. Apparently, to equip Paul for his role, God had permitted His servant some lofty spiritual experiences. In the text Paul speaks of visions, of being lifted up into the heavenlies, of beholding what is ineffable and inexpressible.

It seems that Paul came to view these privileges as a mixed blessing. On the one hand they were a means of strengthening him for the arduous calling that took him across the Roman empire and finally to prison in Rome; but these same visions were, on the other hand, the source of his greatest temptations. Are you aware that our spiritual successes, our lofty moments can be among our greatest dangers? Our life with God is lived in the heart and it is there that our greatest battles take place. When we believe savingly upon Christ, His nature is implanted in us by the new birth. However, our fallen nature, bent and twisted by sin, is present as well.

Paul described the inner warfare in Galatians 5:16–18:

So I say, live by the Spirit, and you will not gratify the desires of the sinful nature. For the sinful nature desires what is contrary to the Spirit, and the Spirit what is contrary to the sinful nature. They are in conflict with each other, so that you do not do what you want. But if you are led by the Spirit, you are not under law.

The secret of the Christian life is not found in endeavoring to improve our old nature. The call of Christ is to take up the cross and follow Him. The cross is not a self-improvement kit, but an instrument of death. Crucifixion is God's answer for the self-life, by our denying its power over us and yielding fully to Christ. The posture of victory is humble trust in the fullness of Christ.

That being the case, our greatest enemy is pride. Whatever causes us to put our confidence in human nature rather than in Christ becomes the enemy's secret weapon. Likewise, a realistic view of my human frailty will keep me resting in the indwelling life of Christ. Spiritual successes and lofty experiences can easily translate into confidence in the flesh. After all, if God thinks enough of me to lift me to visions of glory, then surely I have gained the stature to handle this on my own.

In his beautiful hymn, "The Everlasting Arms," Dr. A.B. Simpson wrote with penetrating insight, "Save us from the strength that harms." The wise man observed that "Pride goes before destruction, a haughty spirit before a fall" (Proverbs 16:18). Understanding this paradox, that one's strength and self-confidence can be an Achilles' heel, will be a means of defense. A common factor in those servants of God who experience moral failure is the belief that it could never happen to them. The strong awareness that it *could* happen to me might well be my greatest defense.

So Paul was caught up to the third heaven. It is easy to imagine what a source of encouragement and inner confidence it must be to experience such delights. The apostle needed such things to strengthen him in a calling that involved unrelenting opposition and buffeting. Yet how could this trusted servant be kept from the self-confidence that destroys? Somehow Paul was enabled to understand this spiritual secret and rightly interpret the thorn which God designed for Paul: "To keep me from becoming conceited because of these surpassingly great revelations, there was given me a thorn in my flesh, a messenger of Satan, to torment me" (2 Corinthians 12:7).

So Paul understood that God had given him a thorn in the flesh to keep him humble. Some kind of infirmity which would constantly remind him of his own inadequacy. The Greek word translated thorn is *skolops* and indicates not the kind of thorn with which you might prick your finger, but rather more like a spear which might pierce your side. It is safe to say it is a fairly noticeable sort of thing!

We do not know exactly what it was, but as you might guess, scholars have suggested a number of possible answers. Some think it was a speech impediment. Some in Corinth had less than complimentary things to say of Paul's preaching and personal appearance: "For some say, 'His letters are weighty and forceful, but in person he is unimpressive and his speaking amounts to nothing' " (10:10). "I may not be a trained speaker, but I do have knowledge" (11:6).

Another idea is that he had poor eyesight and may have been what today would be legally blind. There is at least one reference in his letters (Galatians 6:11) to his handwriting being large. Whatever it was, it seems evident that it made Paul feel inadequate and may have been something that caused people to belittle him.

We can easily understand Paul's conversations with God. "Lord, surely you can see how much more effective I would be without this. I know you have power to take it away. I believe in your goodness. Therefore, Lord, take it!"

Three times the apostle pressed his petition but three times God refused. As he prayed he was in the shadow of his Lord who had likewise prayed in Gethsemane three times, "Father, if you are willing, take this cup from me; yet not my will, but yours be done." (Luke 22:42).

The answer came. It always does, if we are listening. It was not the answer Paul asked for, but it was an answer in line with his heart commitment. Long before, Paul had made the glory of God his first priority. God's answer was in line with that desire.

God's Power Reaches Its Fulfillment in Our Weakness

"My grace is sufficient for you, for my power is made perfect in weakness" (2 Corinthians 12:9).

This letter began by praising the God of all comfort who comforts us in all our troubles so that we may be a comfort to any who are in trouble. The essence of all ministry is the communication of the life of Jesus in the heart of one believer to others who are in need. We observed in the first chapter that Jesus is best seen not in our strengths but in our weaknesses. Here at the end of the letter Paul revisits this same truth. The emphasis now is not so much on the effect of our ministry but on the resource.

The feelings of success are habit-forming, much like a

mood-altering drug. The effects seem so pleasurable and satisfying that we forget that it is only an illusion. Worse yet it anesthetizes the pain of our human weakness and need of God. Unconsciously we are soon in dependence upon the narcotic effect of success rather than upon the reality of God's Spirit. Spiritual successes are no different, only more subtle and dangerous. The adulation of religious people has been the downfall of many a saint.

The spiritual journey may sound something like this: "O God, I love You. I love You, Lord. I love to serve You. Lord, I love to be involved in Your work. I love to do Your work. O Lord, I love Your work. Lord, it brings me great joy to feel successful in Your work. I love to be successful in Your work. O Lord, I love to be successful." Imperceptibly, this person has moved from loving God to loving success. Spiritual effectiveness grows out of our dependence upon God. Our sense of weakness becomes our strength.

In one of our first pastorates I was privileged to have a choice servant of God settle in our community to spend his retirement years. Retired pastors are not always a blessing to a congregation. The unquenched thirst for the heady wine of success may cause insensitivity to the opportunities for true servanthood. It takes a good bit of maturity for a person who has been in leadership to adjust and become an effective follower. I was fortunate to have such a person become not only a faithful congregant but a thoughtful encourager.

This man had been well-known in our denomination as an effective pastor, denominational leader and educator. My temptation to feel insecure by his presence in our congregation was soon put to rest by his gracious spirit and Christlike countenance. He exhibited a peace and quiet joy, a grace and kindness that encouraged spiritual growth. His life had a profound and positive effect upon this young, struggling pastor. There was a spiritual fruitfulness and power in his life that whetted my appetite for more of God.

I remember thinking one day how wonderful it must be to possess such spiritual character and grace. I had little idea how much it had cost. There was a bit of trepidation when he called to make an appointment with me. Perhaps he was aware of some of my many shortcomings, I thought, and was coming to kindly correct me. I was totally unprepared for what took place. He had come to seek my advice and to ask me to pray for his weaknesses.

In our times together I began to fathom the pain and sorrow that had been his lifelong companions and griefs that were still tender scars. I began to see that the confidence one sensed in him was in reality a childlike trust in God. His own inner journey was characterized by a sense of failure and utter dependence upon God. I had admired his long record of apparent success in ministry. My life was being changed by the grace of our risen Lord that was manifest in his weakness. His remembrance still leaves a fragrance upon my life.

The Thorn Is Made Effective by Our Acceptance

"Therefore I will boast all the more gladly about my weaknesses, so that Christ's power may rest on me. That is why, for Christ's sake, I delight in weaknesses, in insults, in hardships, in persecutions, in difficulties. For when I am weak, then I am strong" (12:9b–10).

The story of Job may well be the oldest story that the human race possesses. It is no accident that it is a story of suffering and loss. Job found himself in dire straits. Having lost his wealth, his children and then his health, his wife suggested that he curse God and die. When we find ourselves in difficulty that seems unfair and cannot be changed, the temptation inevitably comes to rebel against God.

Bitterness, self-pity, an accusing, complaining spirit— these are symptoms of a heart struggling with rebellion. Like Job, we do not understand that such demands are the height of pride. Without realizing it we are sitting in judgment upon God's goodness, His motives and His purposes.

"I deserve better treatment than this," we say. We look at others and make comparisons that evoke jealousy and envy. Despair and defeat are not far behind. It was when Job submitted and allowed God to be God, that blessing returned. The "why" question was finally resolved (not fully answered, but resolved) when Job responded with acceptance.

Paul could have found himself in a similar situation. How easily he could have reasoned, "Lord, I've given myself to You. I'm sacrificing and suffering to minister and serve You. Look what I get; poor health, rejection by Your people and circumstances that make me feel inadequate."

Acceptance (allowing God to be God) is an important element in spiritual growth and fruitfulness. However, it is only a first step. Paul responded to his thorn with acceptance but he moved beyond acceptance to praise and gratitude.

At the beginning of this study we observed that Paul's affirmations seem almost masochistic. He boasts of his weaknesses and expresses delight in insults, hardships and persecution. When he accepted the thorn under the sovereign hand of God, he opened the door for that thorn to be a source of strength and power in his life.

A group of students on a summer missions ministry in Spain visited a potter's shop. The vivid imagery of

Jeremiah's visit to the potter's house (Jeremiah 18) predisposes Christians to seek the same experience. They watched with delight as he shaped the wet mud into a vessel on his foot-driven wheel and then placed it in the heated oven. One of the students inquired as to how he would know when to remove it. "I just open the oven and flick the vessel with my finger," said the potter, "and if it sings I know it is ready to come out of the heat."

Paul's witness to us is that while suffering is part of the fallenness of Adam's race, because of redemption we need not be victims but can be victors. Paul's humanness is seen in his petition for the thorn to be removed, but his spiritual maturity is displayed in the yieldedness that allowed his suffering to be a tool for powerful ministry. He had learned to sing in the midst of the heat.

Endnotes

1. Francis A. Schaeffer, *The Church at the End of the Twentieth Century* (Downers Grove: InterVarsity Press, 1970), pp. 110–112.

CHAPTER 14

Put Yourself to the Test

2 Corinthians 13

I have a friend who is into running marathons. When you
meet him he seems no different that the average man
his age. There is nothing about him that would make
you guess that inside his chest cavity there beats a heart that
has been trained by years of exercise and discipline to run
the long race. In fact, if he started in a foot race with the
average man his age they would probably appear about the
same for the first 100 yards or so. Then the inner realities
would begin to make a radical difference. No contest.

Most of our observations of other people are like that. We
view only the externals. We can see the actions and hear the
words and perhaps watch responses to various situations but
we have little idea what goes on inside. It is only on rare
occasions that someone allows us to view the inner person—
the motives, the affections of the heart, the inner struggles,
the doubts and fears that threaten to overwhelm in the midst
of difficulty. We have all observed "successful people" and
assumed that they have it all together, forgetting that in the
inner sanctuary he or she may wrestle with the same fears

and discouragements we do.

Paul's second Corinthian letter affords one of those rare moments. It is a bit like a cardiogram that allows us to read the heartbeat. We have sought to read the letter carefully so as to discern the heartbeat of this passionate lover of God. In this letter written to a congregation where there was a good deal of criticism and opposition, Paul chose to be vulnerable and honest. His openness has given a beautiful gift to successive generations of believers. We have found jewels of insight about the nature of ministry.

It is easy for us to relate to such an open person. Paul struggles with a congregation torn by disagreement. It was really more than that. He was the spiritual father of the believers in Corinth, having preached and introduced the gospel there and seen the church brought to birth under his ministry. He felt a great responsibility for their spiritual nurture and growth.

It was painful to see them divided and scattered by false teachers who had come like wolves among sheep. It was not just their teaching that was false, but also their lives—their attitudes and relationships reflected the error in which they walked. The division, strife and competitive spirit were witness to teaching that was rooted in the flesh.

Paul not only knew the pain of watching his spiritual children devastated by false teachings, but he smarted under a barrage of criticism. The letter alludes to the nature of it:

> He makes a poor impression and his speaking is beneath contempt. (2 Corinthians 10:10)
> He is crude and uncultured in his speech. (11:6)
> He is a fool. (11:16)
> He is dishonest and has defrauded people. (12:16)

Whatever else you might want to say about the critics, they were thorough. There wasn't much that they missed. They attacked his preaching and speaking gifts (a tender spot for any preacher), his intellectual prowess and judgment, even his integrity. That's enough to discourage a fellow, isn't it?

The fire of criticism brings pain but it also brings opportunity for a powerful witness to godliness. The closing paragraphs of Paul's letter leave the reader with a fragrance of maturity and grace. Paul didn't cower before his critics. He was, in fact, bold and firm. But his response kept open the door for ministry. He challenged them to examine their hearts. And the challenge was given in such a spirit as to invite one to do so.

Some years ago, a friend whom I have looked to as a mentor, challenged me to look at every critic as being a messenger from God. The idea is not that the critic is correct or kind or loving, but that the circumstance is an occasion when God has something to say. I accepted his challenge and I have endeavored to do that. His advice has not made criticism painless, but it has on occasion made it profitable. The result is that some of my critics, who have been at best unkind and perhaps even hateful, have been used by God to bring personal growth and understanding. With this attitude in mind, let's reflect on the closing of this second letter to the Corinthian believers.

The letter was written to prepare for another visit of Paul to Corinth. While the earlier visit of Titus had brought repentance on the part of many, Paul was aware that he would find some who were still belligerent and accusatory. We have observed that Paul did not intend to fight with them on a fleshly level, but neither did he intend to ignore their attitudes.

> This will be my third visit to you. "Every matter must be established by the testimony of two or three witnesses." I already gave you a warning when I was with you the second time. I now repeat it while absent: On my return I will not spare those who sinned earlier or any of the others, since you are demanding proof that Christ is speaking through me. He is not weak in dealing with you, but is powerful among you. For to be sure, he was crucified in weakness, yet he lives by God's power. Likewise, we are weak in him, yet by God's power we will live with him to serve you. (13:1–4)

In most letters the closing comments tend to restate the underlying purpose of the letter. A number of the "secrets" of ministry that we observed in Paul's witness now come to bear as the apostle lovingly confronts the attitude issues.

The Authority of Christ

When the Corinthians reacted to Paul's letter of correction by rejecting his leadership and attacking him, the basic issue was authority. Some were saying that Paul was not worthy to be an apostle and his words should not be heeded. He alludes to these accusations in verse 3.

For Paul the answer to the charge was obvious. Christ was present and powerful among them. Through Paul's preaching the church had been born in Corinth and under his teaching the believers had been nurtured. The church there in "sin city" was the result of apostolic ministry. Christ's power among them was evidence that Paul's ministry had been effective. Paul was careful to point out to them that Christ's power among them was born out of his weakness.

It was by Christ's submission to the will of the Father and His death on the cross that the victory over sin had been won and His right established as Head of the Church. And Paul understood in the same way that his authority in Christ was born out of weakness, that is, his willingness to submit to Christ. It is by identification with Christ in His death and resurrection that the authority of the believer is rooted. Notice that Paul saw it not as authority to rule, but to serve.

It seems rare these days to find servants of God who are able to boldly and lovingly confront a fellow believer and call him or her to repentance. It is not surprising that this would be so, what with the negative attitude that prevails in our society toward any and all authority. It used to be a given in our social structure that a certain respect and authority would be granted to those elected or appointed to leadership. Those days are long gone. The individualism that now reigns supreme crowns every person a sovereign in his or her own eyes and enervates any sense of communal or corporate responsibility.

None of this, however, alters the basic reality of ministry. Nothing opens the citadel of the human heart and allows another into the inner sanctuary except the authority of Christ. That authority is not designated to appointed or elected leaders but rests on those who are radically submitted to Christ. It has always been so. It was Paul's submission to Christ that emboldened him to tell the Corinthians that on his return he would not spare those who had sinned earlier nor any of the others. Such a statement standing alone would sound like "fighting words." It is difficult, though, to fight with someone who has the fragrance of the cross upon him. It was in the same spirit that Paul was able to invite them to self-examination.

Call to Self-Examination

> Examine yourselves to see whether you are in the
> faith; test yourselves. Do you not realize that Christ
> Jesus is in you—unless, of course, you fail the test?
> And I trust that you will discover that we have not
> failed the test. Now we pray to God that you will
> not do anything wrong. Not that people will see that
> we have stood the test but that you will do what is
> right even though we may seem to have failed.
> (13:5–7)

Hear the word of warning about self-deceit. One of the
most subtle forms of self-deceit is that of equating our ability
to see the faults of others with being virtuous. I remember
with no minor embarrassment the expertise I had cultivated
as a college freshman to be a critic. My roommate in the
dorm was a brilliant and witty young man and we led each
other into a pattern of dissecting the lives of people to
uncover their inconsistencies and poke holes in their
theological systems. We were good at it. Both of us had
grown up with a fairly good background in Scripture (knowing just about enough to make us dangerous) and among
our peers we were a force to be reckoned with.

Our arrogant and offensive style no doubt wounded a lot
of people. The real danger, though, was what it was doing
to us. It seemed so natural to believe that individuals who
were so keen at perceiving the faults, sins and phoniness of
others must surely be on the right path. It was a painful day
when God knocked me down and turned the searchlight of
revelation upon my heart to uncover the emptiness, dryness

and dishonesty that characterized my inner life.

It was time for me to turn my investigative skills to look inward. Spiritual blindness is an awful condition. Our impatience and strong reactions to others' faults are often a symptom of blindness about our own condition. That's why Paul challenged them to test themselves. It was their opinion that Paul would not pass the test. He humbly asserted his hope that they would find that he had not failed the test, but that even if he had, the crucial issue for them was whether they had failed it. It seems to me that the apostle did not have doubts about how they might fare in the test, but he was concerned that they get things in focus.

Perhaps Paul's invitation could be a powerful impetus for you at this juncture in your life. So let me challenge you. Examine yourself—are you living in the faith? Put yourself to the test. Do you recognize that Christ Jesus is in you?

Christ in You Is the Issue

Self-examination is healthy when Jesus Christ is the focus. The Puritans believed in self-examination, and they practiced it. They believed in getting alone with God and surveying their lives in His presence with an unsparing scrutiny. We find it a bit difficult to deal with that idea. Modern believers tend to fill their lives with ceaseless activity and avoid quietness or inner reflection like the plague. We may be willing to stand up to the test of doctrinal correctness and perhaps even behavioral righteousness but concerns about the heart seem too other-worldly. We rarely take the time to silence the inner noise and listen to our hearts.

In this letter Paul would want to tell us two things. First, the battleground of faith is the arena of the heart. Second, the basic heart issue is our relationship to Jesus Christ. Plato observed that the unexamined life is not worth living. The Scriptures would agree but the writers would want us to understand that introspection may not necessarily be a healthy activity. Let's talk about that.

David, the man after God's own heart, invited God to search him: "Search me, O God, and know my heart; test me and know my anxious thoughts. See if there is any offensive way in me, and lead me in the way everlasting" (Psalm 139:23–24).

It may sound contradictory at first, but the Scriptures would affirm that self-examination is something that we cannot do ourselves. In fact, most of the saints would counsel us that introspection may be unproductive and should not be attempted alone. Walking down the corridors of your inner life without God could prove destructive.

Remember that Jeremiah said, "The heart is deceitful above all things and beyond cure. Who can understand it?" (17:9). That realization ought to give us pause before we dig too deeply alone. There are insights about human tendencies and behavior to be gained by psychology, but no one can fathom the depths of our fallenness nor our ability to deceive ourselves. The truth is that we cannot know our own motives and we are so weak that we can't change what we do know.

Searching is God's work. Psalm 139:13 declares that God formed us in our mother's womb and knew us then and understands our hearts. Not only does He know us but He has power to change us. In a sense, then, self-examination is an invitation for God to search us and to give us the power to save us from ourselves.

What is it we are looking for in this search? Jesus Christ! Is Jesus Christ living in you now? That's the answer. Does it surprise you? Did you think that self-examination was about searching out your sins, naming them and cataloging them, and then working out a strategy to get rid of them? Such a journey is a road to despair.

The search is for Jesus Christ. If I am in the faith then Jesus Christ lives in me. When I recognize His presence and open my heart to His holiness and purity I will be well aware of my sin. Such an encounter will uncover specific sins that I have committed and wrongs that need to be confessed and made right. Our gentle and loving Lord will not overwhelm us with more than we can handle but He will reveal enough to keep calling us to integrity. The focus is not our sin but Christ. Sin itself, the principle and power of iniquity, I am helpless against. I cannot plumb the depths of it or root it out. God will let me see enough to drive me into the arms of Christ to revel in His redeeming love. It will also help me walk with humility and a forgiving spirit among my fellow men.

From the Puritans we can learn a lot about the discipline of self-examination. Below is a list of the kinds of questions they might have used in putting themselves to the test. These questions will not be very helpful if we use them to walk the corridors of our hearts alone. Such will perhaps only increase our feelings of defeat and despair. However, if we use them to uncover the presence of Christ in us and to quicken our responsiveness and dependence upon Him, they will be an exercise toward spiritual growth.

1. Am I consciously or unconsciously creating the impression that I am a better person than I really am? In other words, am I a hypocrite?

2. Am I honest in all my acts or words, or do I exaggerate?

3. Do I confidentially pass on to another what was told to me in confidence?

4. Can I be trusted?

5. Am I a slave to dress, friends, work or habits?

6. Am I self-conscious, self-pitying or self-justifying? Do I grumble or complain constantly?

7. Did the Bible live for me today?

8. Am I enjoying prayer? Is Christ real to me?

9. When did I last speak to someone else with the object of trying to win that person for Christ?

10. Am I making contacts with other people and using them for the Master's glory?

11. Do I pray about the money I spend?

12. Do I get to bed on time and get up on time?

13. Do I disobey God in anything?

14. Do I insist upon doing something about which my conscience is uneasy?

15. Am I defeated in any part of my life? Am I jealous, impure, critical, irritable, touchy, distrustful?

16. How do I spend my spare time?

17. Am I proud?

18. Do I thank God that I am not as others, especially as the Pharisee who despised the publican?

19. Is there anybody whom I fear, dislike, disown, criticize? What am I doing about it?

As I have read through this exercise it occurs to me that these questions would be devastating to me if I walked through them in my own strength or viewed them as a measurement of my acceptance with God. But as a recipient of great grace through the saving work of Christ there is instead a response of hope. Just a few moments of reflection on these questions began to put me in touch with my inner life. There are a number of hopeful things that came into focus. Let me recount them for you.

1. I can see right away that I am not yet where I ought to be. But at the same time by God's grace I am not where I once was. The reflection brings clear evidence that Christ is at work in my life and that while I am not yet perfect, I am being perfected by His power.
2. I am awakened to new longings for Christ to be formed in me. I am surprised at how strong my spiritual desires are and how much they have been buried and stilled by trivial pursuits.
3. I find myself looking with greater sensitivity and understanding at fellow pilgrims who with me are walking the road to the "celestial city." The fresh awareness of boundless grace takes the edge off my quickness to criticize.

It is good advice that Paul gives. Put yourself to the test so that you may recognize that Christ is in you. It was in his first letter to the Corinthian believers that Paul wrote one of the great biblical statements of Christ's sufficiency: "It is because of him that you are in Christ Jesus, who has become for us wisdom from God—that is, our righteousness, holiness and redemption" (1:30).

I recall a luminous moment that happened in a college Sunday school class that I was teaching. One young woman raised her hand and made a statement that I think was intended to bait me: "Pastor, if Christ is the answer then what is the question?" I can't recall how well I responded at the moment but out of the encounter I came to see that Paul's declaration was what she needed to hear:

- The question is, who am I and what is the meaning of existence? What is good and worth pursuing? How can I find wisdom? The answer is Jesus Christ living within me.
- The question is, how can I be right with God? How can my load of guilt and sin be removed? How can my conscience be at peace? The answer is Jesus Christ living within me.
- The question is, how can I conquer sin and its power over me? How can I find freedom to do what I ought? How can the bonds of habits be broken? The answer is Jesus Christ living in me.
- The question is, how can I have hope in the midst of the decay and corruption that plagues the world? How can the hatred and alienation that corrodes life on planet Earth ever be brought to resolution? The answer is that Jesus Christ will someday return and bring redemption to all creation. And it is a sure and settled hope because we have the down payment in the indwelling presence of Christ.

Paul's restatement of his purpose for writing the letter (13:10) encapsulates his attitude toward authority, the apostolic authority bestowed by Christ Himself. He wrote the letter, he said, so that when he came in person there would not have to be an encounter involving a harsh use of authority. Then he gave the clincher: "the authority the Lord gave me for building you up, not for tearing you down."

This is a fitting capstone for a letter that has so much to say about ministry. God has called every believer to the ministry. He has chosen us to be vessels of blessing and comfort to needy people. He comforts us, says Paul in chapter 1, in all our troubles so that we may be a comfort to any who are in trouble with the comfort that we have received from God. We have gained a good many insights about God's gracious working from this lovely letter, but what could be more basic than this closing reminder that our ministry is given to us by Christ and is not for tearing people down but for building them up? Simply committing ourselves to those two ideas could revolutionize the life of the local church.

When we receive a personal letter it is not uncommon for us to look at the conclusion first. The closing salutation can influence the way the rest of the letter is interpreted. A few brief comments of affection and warmth in the end can imbue the whole letter with a loving fragrance. The New Testament letters are no different. While the authors made use of familiar words of greeting, those terms were infused with special meaning to the children of grace.

It is not only affection that is expressed in the conclusion of a letter but also personal concern. Parental letters will typically have exhortations like "Take care of yourself," "Get plenty of rest" and "Wear your overshoes when it snows!"

Feel the pulse of Paul's pastoral heart and let God speak words of warmth and personal concern to you:

"Aim for perfection" (13:11b)—don't be distracted by lesser things. Keep God's high purposes in view. "Listen to my appeal" (13:11c)—cultivate a quiet heart. Learn to read the Scriptures not with an eye for information but an ear to listen.

"Be of one mind" (13:11d)—bring your drivenness under divine discipline so that the needs and ideas of others take precedence.

"Live in peace" (13:11e)—in God's economy, people are more important than projects. Relationships are the arena in which ministry happens.

"Greet one another with a holy kiss" (13:12)—there are occasions when love is volitional but there is no substitute for affection. In the synagogue men and women were segregated. Men embraced men— women embraced women. Apparently the early church followed the same custom. When I attend a social club I expect a handshake, but when I am among believers I expect that and more.

And as you go, "The God of love and peace will be with you" (13:11f). "May the grace of the Lord Jesus Christ, and the love of God, and the fellowship of the Holy Spirit be with you all" (13:14).

Amen!

BIBLIOGRAPHY

Adizes, Ichak. *Corporate Lifecycles: How and Why Corporations Grow and Die and What to Do About It.* Englewood Cliffs, NJ: Prentice-Hall, 1988.

Aldrich, Joseph. *Lifestyle Evangelism.* Portland, OR: Multnomah Press, 1981.

Benson, Ben. *Come Share the Being.* Nashville: Impact Books, 1974.

Crabb, Larry. *Inside Out.* Colorado Springs, CO: Navpress, 1988.

Lewis, C.S. *The Problem of Pain.* New York: MacMillan, 1962.

Lewis, C.S. *The Weight of Glory.* Grand Rapids, MI: Eerdmans, 1949.

McLuhan, Marshall, and Quentin Fiore. *The Medium Is the Message.* New York: Random House, 1967.

Nouwen, Henri. *Creative Ministry.* Garden City, NY: Nelson Doubleday, 1971.

Schaeffer, Francis A. *The Church at the End of the Twentieth Century.* Downers Grove, IL: InterVarsity Press, 1970.

Winter, Ralph. "Editorial." *Mission Frontiers: Bulletin of the U.S. Center for World Evangelism. March-April, 1992,* p. 4.